DISCARDED

DAILY LIFE

Games of Ancient Rome

Don Nardo

KIDHAVEN PRESS

An imprint of Thomson Gale, a part of The Thomson Corporation

THOMSON

GALE

Detroit • New York • San Francisco • San Diego • New Haven, Conn.
Waterville, Maine • London • Munich

© 2005 Thomson Gale, a part of The Thomson Corporation.

Thomson and Star Logo are trademarks and Gale and KidHaven Press are registered trademarks used herein under license.

For more information, contact
KidHaven Press
27500 Drake Rd.
Farmington Hills, MI 48331-3535
Or you can visit our Internet site at http://www.gale.com

LIBRARY OF CONGRESS CATALOGING-IN-PUBLICATION DATA
Nardo, Don, 1947-
Games of ancient Rome / by Don Nardo.
p. cm. — (Daily life)
Includes bibliographical references and index.
ISBN 0-7377-2345-9 (hardcover : alk. paper)
1. Games—Rome—Juvenile literature. 2. Games—History—Juvenile literature. I. Title. II. Series.
GV31.N37 2005
790'.0937—dc22
2004018200

Contents

CHAPTER ONE

The Arena Fighters

Most people today would be horrified if the most popular sporting events regularly ended with people being mangled and killed. But, this was the usual fare in the public games in ancient Rome. Building on centuries of tradition, the Romans greatly enjoyed bloody spectator sports.

As often as possible these fans crowded into huge stone stadiums called **amphitheaters.** There they cheered and jeered as they watched trained fighters—the gladiators—attack one another with swords, spears, daggers, and nets. Inevitably, blood was spilled. And the sands of the **arena** (the flat area in the center of the amphitheater) turned from light brown to bright red. Other arena fighters, called "hunters," grappled with wild animals, including tigers, bears, and elephants. The hunters also goaded the animals into fighting one another.

The Romans enjoyed other large-scale spectator sports as well, including chariot racing. This event took place in long oval racetracks called **circuses,** in which the charioteers drove their teams of horses at breakneck speeds. Sometimes they crashed, killing both men and horses. Still another popular public game consisted of staged naval battles. These fights featured full-sized ships with crews of sailors who fought to the death as crowds of onlookers urged them on.

Slaves, Criminals, and Volunteers

It is only natural to wonder who these arena fighters were and why and how they ended up having either to kill or be killed in violent public displays. Not surprisingly, most of them had no choice. The majority of

This is how Rome's greatest amphitheater, the Colosseum, looked during the early centuries of the Roman Empire.

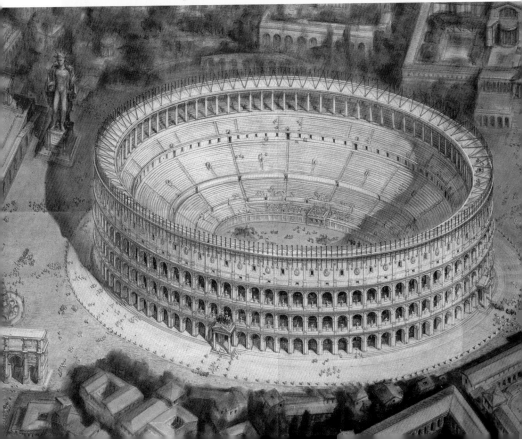

Gladiators were often popular with young women. Here, several women gather around a fighter after his victory.

these warriors were not free persons. Many were slaves, who had no rights and could be bought and sold like property. Others were criminals or war captives. All of these unfortunate individuals were simply forced to fight in the public games. (Some of the lucky ones who managed to survive numerous fights eventually earned or bought their freedom. But they were definitely in the minority.)

On the other hand, a few of the fighters were free individuals who volunteered to enter the arena. One reason they did so was the lure of money. Well-to-do people who owned groups of these fighters sometimes offered hefty bonuses to free persons with the guts to sign up. Also, the managers of the games, which were at first privately financed and run, often gave prize money to those who won their bouts and pleased the crowds.

Other volunteers were attracted by the physical challenge of battling for their lives. Still others signed up because many Romans looked on such fighting as manly. So a gladiator had a chance of becoming a star who could have his pick of pretty young girls. Someone painted the following messages on a wall in the Roman town of Pompeii: "Caladus, the Thracian [a kind of gladiator], makes all the girls sigh," and "Crescens, the net fighter, holds the hearts of all the girls."[1]

Rounding Up the Recruits

At first, those Romans who owned gladiators and other arena fighters bought them from a special dealer called a **lanista**. He traveled from place to place searching for slaves or prisoners he could buy cheaply. Sometimes he

A *lanista* (left) talks with gladiators in his stable of fighters in this scene from the Oscar-winning movie *Gladiator*.

attended slave auctions held in town squares. He might also purchase slaves from private owners trying to make some extra cash. More disreputable lanistae obtained slaves from pirates. It was not unusual for a pirate band to raid a village or farm and kidnap everyone who lived there. (Whether the lanistae dealt with pirates or not, most Romans looked down them as shady and sleazy characters.)

This means of getting recruits for the arenas changed significantly in the era of the famous military general Julius Caesar. (Caesar lived in the first century B.C., a little over two thousand years ago.) By this time, the public games had become extremely large-scale and popular, and the Roman government took over running them.

The government rounded up slaves and prisoners for the games in some of the same ways the lanistae did. However, the government was much more efficient than ordinary slave merchants. When the Romans won a battle against a foreign people, for example, they captured hundreds or thousands of enemy fighters. The healthiest and strongest of these prisoners became arena fighters. The government also created a special penalty for some crimes. Some people convicted of murder, arson, treason, or other serious crimes were forced to become gladiators.

A Strange Double Standard

Because so many gladiators and other arena fighters were slaves and criminals, most Romans looked down on them socially. Such a person was commonly viewed

Some gladiators had families. This painting shows the concerned wife of a man forced to fight to death in the arena.

as vulgar, crude, and worthless. In fact, all arena fighters had to live with the knowledge that they were at the bottom of the social ladder. As one Roman writer put it, "There is no meaner condition among the people than that of the gladiator."[2] Certainly the average Roman would be shocked and horrified if his or her daughter married a gladiator.

It was considered even worse for someone's son to marry a gladiator. There were women gladiators, too, although they were far less common than the male versions. Socially speaking, most people viewed the female gladiator, or gladiatrix, as scandalous and vile. The popular Roman poet and humorist Juvenal made fun of what he called "our lady-fencers." He asked:

What modesty can be looked for in some helmeted vixen [wicked girl] . . . who thrives on

Found in Turkey, this carving shows two female gladiators. Their names—Amazonia and Achillia—appear below them.

masculine violence? . . . What a fine sight for some husband—*it might be you*—his wife's equipment put up at auction, sword-belt . . . plumes [helmet decorations], and one odd shin-guard![3]

The Romans had a strange double standard about gladiators, however. In spite of the low social status of these fighters, both male and female, once they entered the arena their negative image changed completely. People admired their exploits with swords and other weapons. And those who won often became popular heroes like today's biggest football, baseball, and basketball stars. A few of these warriors earned their freedom. Meanwhile, a handful became rich from both their winnings and the gifts adoring fans showered on them.

Yet fame and money usually gave little comfort to these fighters when they retired. Few people wanted a former arena fighter in the family. So retired gladiators had difficulty finding wives and husbands. Some people shunned them on the streets and in the marketplace. What is more, gladiators were not allowed to be buried in public cemeteries. Only when a relative, friend, or loyal fan claimed the body and buried it privately did a retired arena fighter get a proper funeral.

In ancient Rome, therefore, gladiators were cheered one minute and rejected the next. And all the while, the threat of sudden and brutal death hung over them. Clearly, theirs was not a lifestyle to be envied in any age or place.

CHAPTER TWO

Training for a Dangerous Job

When a gladiator or other fighter entered the arena, it was crucial that he or she employ as much strength and skill as possible. On the one hand, the fighter desperately wanted to survive the bout. On the other, it was his or her duty to put on a good show for the crowd. Spectators often booed or demanded the death of fighters who were not giving it their all.

For these reasons, the gladiators went through rigorous training to prepare themselves for their duels to the death. The training took place in special schools called **ludi.** There, the recruits endured months or years of harsh discipline and relentless drills. During the training their lives were very rigidly ordered, and they had to do exactly as they were told at all times.

Gladiator Schools

During the age of the Roman Empire (around 30 B.C.–A.D. 476), the city of Rome had four ludi. Three of them trained gladiators, while the fourth prepared the animal fighters the Romans called "hunters." The biggest and most important of these schools was the Ludus Magnus. It was located near the Colosseum, the empire's largest and most famous amphitheater. The school and Colosseum were connected by an underground tunnel. This let the fighters move from one facility to the other without being seen by the public.

This illustration shows the barracks and small arena at Rome's most famous gladiator school, the Ludus Magnus.

However, the raw recruits had much to learn before they would be allowed to fight in the mighty Colosseum. Their training fights took place in a small arena located inside the Ludus Magnus itself. The seating capacity was about three thousand (as compared to fifty thousand for the Colosseum). Interested citizens were sometimes allowed to sit and watch the gladiators train, in the same way that modern baseball fans watch the players during spring training.

The trainees lived in small rooms called cells inside a three-story-high structure built around the edges of the arena. Most parts of this building no longer exist. But some idea of what it was like can be seen at Pompeii. That town, which was very well preserved by the lava from a large volcanic eruption, had its own gladiator school. The Pompeian ludus had almost a hundred brick cells grouped around a rectangular training area. Each cell was only a few feet long and wide and had no windows. The cell had no decorations. And the only furniture was perhaps an uncomfortable cot for the trainee to sleep on.

A Hard and Repetitive Routine

The official who ran the school—called a **procurator**— did not care about the recruits' comforts or feelings. His job was to turn out as many tough and skilled fighters as possible. To this end, he exercised total authority over all aspects of the trainees' lives. The procurator decided when and how long they drilled, what and when they ate, and how long they slept. He also punished them when they broke the rules. Disorderly

The remains of the gladiator school at Pompeii include the central training grounds, where recruits drilled every day.

trainees were usually placed in the school's prison. This was a stinking, stone-lined hole where inmates had to wear painful chains and lie on their backs in the dark for several days or more.

The trainees learned the rules when they first arrived at the school. First they took part in a formal ceremony in which they swore the gladiatorial oath. The exact words are unknown. But they likely went something like this: "I swear to be burned, to be bound, to be beaten, [and] to die by the sword."

After this ceremony, the recruits began a hard and repetitive routine that would last for months or years. The only times they were allowed outside their cells were when they were training and eating. At mealtimes, armed guards led them to the school's kitchen. It featured a large stone hearth on which cooks heated food in big metal pots. The food was hearty and the

An instructor shows trainees where to strike on the body in this scene from the 1960 film Spartacus.

trainees could eat all they wanted. After all, the main aim of the school was to produce healthy, strong fighters.

Tight Security Measures

Armed guards also stood around the edges of the training grounds while the recruits were learning to fight. In addition, it was strictly against the rules for the trainees to possess weapons when they were away from the training area. This included knives, cleavers, and other kitchen tools that might be used as weapons. Such tight security measures were vital. Most of the inmates were strong, determined men who did not want to be there and would jump at any chance to escape.

In fact, if several trainees escaped at the same time the consequences could be serious. All Romans were haunted by the memory of what they called the "War of Spartacus." In 73 B.C. some gladiators escaped from a privately run ludus in a town not far from Pompeii. The first-century A.D. Greek writer Plutarch said that they were "armed with [meat] choppers . . . which they seized from [the] cookhouse." But soon they got their hands on better weapons: "On the road they came across some wagons which were carrying arms for gladiators to another city, and they took these arms for their own use."[4]

Led by a man named Spartacus, the gladiators freed many other slaves, trained them, and thereby created an army. That powerful force defeated several small Roman armies. And this sent a wave of fear throughout Italy. Eventually, though, the rebels were defeated and all were killed.

Relentless Drills

Thanks to the guards keeping a close watch on the recruits as they trained, no other such mass escapes occurred. Under the guards' gaze, the daily training was supervised by instructors. Each taught a particular kind of weapon or fighting style. Some were experts with swords. Others drilled the recruits in the effective use of spears, nets, or shields.

In the early stages of training, the recruits attacked a six-foot-tall wooden pole. Using a wooden sword they struck at the pole, pretending it was a human opponent. Over and over, they drilled in the basic moves of attack and defense. When the instructors felt they were ready, the trainees began using real swords against each other (but the tips were blunt).

In this old engraving, the famous gladiator Spartacus leads a huge slave rebellion in the first century B.C.

These reenactors are demonstrating some of the moves of ancient gladiators. Here, they strike at a palus (pole).

During the weeks and months of intensive drills, minor injuries sometimes occurred. In such cases the inmates were fortunate, for some of the best physicians worked in the ludi. (Galen, the finest doctor in Rome's history, began his career tending the wounds of gladiators.) There was a good reason for this excellent medical care. The Roman government had a lot of money invested in the training of arena fighters. And it viewed them as valuable property that must be well maintained. It is striking that those individuals the Romans looked down on the most had the best health care available—and for free!

CHAPTER THREE

The Fight to the Death

Sooner or later, all gladiator trainees had to face the moment of truth. When the officials at a gladiator school felt that certain recruits were ready, they assigned them to fight in an upcoming **munus.** This is the Latin word the Romans used to describe a gladiatorial show. Large-scale munera (the plural of munus) were very expensive to stage. So, with some exceptions, they took place only on public holidays. On those occasions the seats at the Colosseum and other amphitheaters were jam-packed with eager fans.

A typical munus began with a colorful parade. Just as the spectators cheered, the fighters marched into the arena, along with jugglers, acrobats, and other performers. All stepped or danced to lively music played by trumpets, flutes, drums, and sometimes a large organ.

Following this pre-game show, the acrobats and other minor performers departed. Then the gladiators drew lots (random tokens from a container) to decide who would fight whom. Next, the manager of the munus inspected the fighters' weapons to make sure they were sound and well sharpened. Finally, the fighters saluted the highest-ranking officials in the stands and shouted the phrase "Those who are about to die salute you!"

Various Combat Strategies

After these ceremonies, the actual combats began. As a rule, the men (and on occasion women) fought in pairs.

Gladiators march during the colorful parade that opened the typical gladiator show. Fewer marched out than marched in.

Contrary to what is shown in movies like *Gladiator*, fights involving large groups of gladiators were fairly rare. Also, movies fail to show the referees who oversaw the bouts. Usually there were two for each fight, a main referee and his assistant. The fighters had to follow strict rules (which are not very well understood today). And a referee could stop a fight at any time. He could allow the fighters to rest for a few minutes, have a doctor tend to a small wound, or use a stick to beat a gladiator who had broken a rule.

As a referee watches closely, a heavily armed fighter attacks a retiarius who has lost his net.

The combat the referees oversaw was strenuous and often bloody. The actual moves the fighters made depended a great deal on how they were armed. There were many different types of gladiator, each of which had distinct armor and weapons. One common type, the **myrmillo**, carried a sword and a large rectangular (or oval) shield. He wore a metal helmet and protective armor on one arm. His name, meaning "fish man," came from a fish-shaped crest that adorned his helmet. His strategy was to use his sword to wound or kill his opponent.

Another common and popular kind of gladiator was often paired with the myrmillo. Called a **retiarius** ("net man"), he carried a net and a three-pronged spear and wore no armor at all. His strategy was to ensnare his opponent in the net and then stab him with the spear. According to an ancient source, one fight between a fish man and a net man ended with the myrmillo running away. The retiarius supposedly yelled, "It is not you I am trying to catch, it's your fish! Why do you run away?"[5]

Other gladiators used different kinds of weapons, tactics, and attack strategies. Some wielded two swords (or daggers), one in each hand. Others fought on horseback or from moving chariots and either threw or jabbed with spears. Still others twirled a lasso, like that of American cowboys, with which they tripped or entangled their opponents and then choked them. A few gladiator types were offbeat. In one downright weird confrontation, two fighters grappled while blindfolded by large helmets with no eyeholes.

This mosaic, found in a Roman town in North Africa, shows a number of common gladiator types.

Win, Lose, or Draw

No matter what the armor, weapons, and strategies of the fighters, their bouts had a number of common and expected outcomes. One was when someone won by either killing or seriously wounding his opponent. A wounded fighter who had fallen was not allowed to move or to touch his weapons. If he did grab for a weapon, the crowd booed and cursed him. And the manager of the games could order him killed immediately.

The fallen gladiator was allowed to raise one finger, which was seen as an appeal for mercy. The manager (or the emperor if he happened to be there) decided the poor fellow's fate, usually following the wishes of the spectators. The traditional view is that a thumbs-up meant "spare him" and a thumbs-down "kill him." But some experts think this is wrong. They suggest that a thumbs-down was the sign for the victor to drop his sword and spare the loser. And to signal their desire for a death sentence, the spectators pressed their thumbs toward their chests (a "sword-through-the-heart" gesture).

Another common outcome of the bouts was a draw. It usually happened when both warriors had fought bravely for a long time and neither could beat the other. In a draw, each combatant received a prize (a palm branch or money, or sometimes both). The popular Roman poet Martial recorded just such a situation:

> As Priscus and Verus each drew out the contest and the struggle between the pair long stood equal, [the crowd demanded that the match be declared a draw]. Equal they fought, equal they

Pointing their thumbs down, the crowd calls for death in this French painting.

yielded. To both, [the emperor] sent . . . [victory palms]. Thus valor and skill had their reward.[6]

Other outcomes were possible as well. On occasion, the manager or another official ordered that no draws be allowed. In such cases, the gladiators had to keep fighting until one was dead, no matter how long it took. There were also times when both the officials and the spectators felt the fighters were not trying hard enough. If so, one or both men (or women) might be whipped or branded with hot irons. Even worse was when one combatant turned and ran for his life. His punishment was whipping, branding, or immediate execution. Finally, on very rare occasions a fallen fighter pretended to be dead. But this strategy never worked. Men dressed like demons ran out and applied

At the end of a gladiator show, victorious gladiators stand among the bodies of the losers.

hot irons to the bodies. This exposed any fakers, who quickly had their throats cut.

The Beast Shows

Gladiators were not the only ones who stained the arena sands with their blood. The animal hunters and their prey also thrilled crowds by fighting to the death. A wild beast show was usually presented just before the gladiatorial bouts in an amphitheater.

The most common weapon wielded by the hunters was the spear. However, these fighters sometimes used swords, daggers, clubs, lassos, and bows and arrows. They also used their bare hands. Some hunters wrestled bulls to the ground before stabbing them with swords or spears. Once the hunters began to attack them, the confused and frightened animals had nowhere to run or hide. Many of the beasts fought back, and on occasion they managed to kill one of their human pursuers. But all the animals died in the end.

Hunters, who were really low-level gladiators, attack and kill wild animals in one of the popular beast shows.

In addition to these slaughters, the Romans enjoyed other sorts of beast shows. In one, trained animals performed tricks. Sometimes monkeys dressed as soldiers drove miniature chariots drawn by goats. And lions held rabbits and cats in their jaws without harming them. In still another kind of beast show, half-starved animals attacked unarmed prisoners who had been condemned to death. Clearly, the Roman arena was a place where lighthearted fun, terror, and sudden death combined in ways that today are difficult to grasp.

CHAPTER FOUR

Chariot Races and Staged Naval Battles

Although the Romans loved gladiatorial fights and wild beast shows, they loved chariot racing even more. In fact, the chariot races were the most popular spectator sport throughout Rome's long history. These races were grander in scale than the amphitheater attractions.

This was partly because the circuses—the facilities where the races took place—were huge. The famous Circus Maximus, in Rome, was the largest single structure the Romans ever built. It was one-third of a mile (0.5 km) long and 150 yards (117 m) in width. Its arena was twelve times bigger than that of the Colosseum, and its stands held at least 150,000 people!

Incredibly, the spectacles presented in the Circus Maximus were dwarfed by another kind of public show-the **naumachiae.** These were full-scale sea battles. Most often they took place on lakes, both real and artificial. (Experts still debate whether these shows were ever held in flooded amphitheaters.) The sea fights were tremendously expensive to stage. So they

A modern painting captures the excitement as the lead chariot teams round the far end of Rome's Circus Maximus.

occurred rather infrequently. Chariot races took place in the Circus Maximus on as many as fifteen to twenty days each year. But a naumachia occurred only once every few years.

The Fans and Drivers

Romans of all walks of life looked forward to these events. On those days when races were scheduled in the Circus Maximus, for instance, immense crowds gathered early in the day. Attendance was free, but seating was on a first-come, first-served basis. Many of the fans stayed to see all the races. There were twenty-four races per day, and sitting on stone seats for many hours could be uncomfortable. So the spectators used cushions that they either carried with them or rented at the circus. Many nibbled on food they brought from home or purchased at snack bars located beneath the stands.

The fans cheered and applauded loudly when the charioteers entered the arena. These drivers were a mix of slaves and free persons. If they won often enough, even the slaves became widely popular sports heroes. Each popular driver and his team of horses gathered a loyal following—hundreds or thousands of fans who supported him at every race.

The cheers of the crowd were not the only rewards that successful charioteers enjoyed. There was also prize money for the winners. The owners of the teams (and the drivers, if they were slaves) received the victory purses. But they shared the money with their winning drivers.

In this way, some drivers became extremely rich. Juvenal joked, "You'll find that a hundred lawyers scarcely make more [money] than one successful jockey."[7] Indeed, one of Rome's most successful charioteers, Calpurnianus, won 1,127 victories. Several of these paid him about forty times the annual wage of a Roman soldier. Another popular charioteer, Diocles, erected a monument to record his victories and winnings. It said in part:

He drove four-horse chariots for 24 years. He had . . . 1,462 first-place finishes . . . winning 92 major purses, 32 of them worth 30,000 sesterces [equivalent to many thousands of dollars today]. . . . In 815 races, he took the lead at the start and held it to the end. In 67 races, he came from behind to win.[8]

On-Track Warfare

Four-horse chariots like the ones Diocles drove were the most common. But there were also chariots drawn

In a scene from the 1959 film version of *Ben-Hur*, chariots race while huge crowds cheer them on.

by two, three, six, or eight horses. In addition, these shows featured different kinds of races. In the standard version, the drivers sped around and around a long, statue-covered stone structure that ran down the middle of the track. They had to complete seven full laps (about two and a half miles, or four kilometers). In a less common but still popular race, two men stood in one chariot. When the vehicle crossed the finish line, one of them jumped out. And as the crowd cheered loudly, he sprinted at top speed once around the track.

When it was time for the first race to begin, four to twelve drivers and their teams took their positions in the starting gates. At this point a sudden hush fell over the

A nineteenth-century painting depicts a charioteer (right) trying to hold his lead on the inside lane.

crowded circus. From his seat, located just above the starting gates, the manager of the races (or the emperor if he was present) tossed out a white cloth. As it touched the track, attendants released a cord that held the fronts of the gates in place. Instantly, the horses leaped forward and a mighty roar erupted from the stands.

As the race progressed, the drivers tried to gain every possible advantage. In particular, each attempted to reach the inside lane. The distance of a lap in this position was a little shorter than in the outer lanes. To gain this edge, the drivers often resorted to ruthless and violent means. It was not unusual for one charioteer to break a rival's wheels or slash at him with a whip.

Sometimes this on-track warfare caused a chariot and its horses to crash into a hideous mass of twisted debris and broken bones. The Romans called it a "shipwreck." At other times, a chariot crashed but the horses continued on, dragging the unlucky driver behind them. This happened partly because it was customary for drivers to wind their reins around their waists. To escape such a situation, a driver tried to draw a dagger and cut himself free of the reins.

No Escape

The chances of dying were even higher for the participants of staged naval battles. Manning the warships in these spectacles were criminals and war captives. They took on the roles of sailors and soldiers in rival fleets, usually in re-creations of famous naval battles of the past. One very popular and often repeated one was the Battle of Salamis, fought in 480 B.C. between the Greeks and the Persians.

Although some naumachiae took place on lakes, sometimes an emperor ordered the digging and flooding of a special basin. The first emperor, Augustus, did this in 2 B.C. "I presented to the people an exhibition of a naval battle," he later wrote, in an "excavated [lake] 1,800 feet in length and 1,200 feet in width."[9]

One driver lashes a whip at another in this shot from the exciting chariot race from *Ben-Hur* (1959).

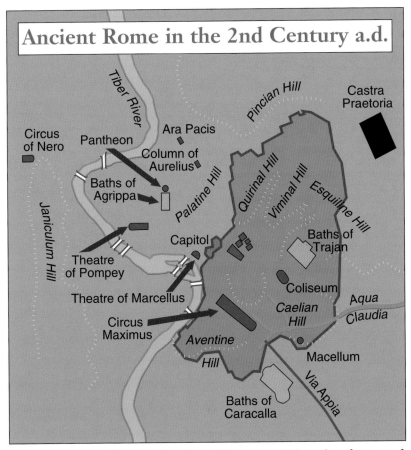

Ancient Rome in the 2nd Century a.d.

Tiber River

Pincian Hill

Castra Praetoria

Circus of Nero

Pantheon

Ara Pacis

Column of Aurelius

Baths of Agrippa

Palatine Hill

Quirinal Hill

Viminal Hill

Esquiline Hill

Janiculum Hill

Capitol

Baths of Trajan

Theatre of Pompey

Theatre of Marcellus

Coliseum

Aqua Claudia

Caelian Hill

Circus Maximus

Aventine Hill

Macellum

Via Appia

Baths of Caracalla

Augustus bragged that his naval battle featured more than thirty ships, with crews totaling three thousand men. These sailor-fighters first tried to maneuver their vessels so they could ram other ships. The ships had metal beaks mounted on their fronts, so if a ramming was successful, the enemy ship sank. The participants also boarded opposing ships and fought hand to hand. Most or all were eventually killed. Unfortunately for them, there was no escape because thousands of Roman soldiers stood guard on the outer edges of the lake.

Over time, these spectacles became too expensive to put on. The government discontinued them. Also, in the last century of Rome's existence, the Romans shut down gladiatorial fights. By this time, all of the high-placed government officials were Christians who viewed these events as murder. The chariot races lasted a good deal longer. But they, too, eventually became too expensive to stage. As the centuries passed, weeds and rubble slowly filled the empty amphitheaters and circuses. And the vast public games that had thrilled millions of devoted fans over many generations became only a fleeting memory.

Notes

Chapter One: The Arena Fighters

1. Quoted in Jo-Ann Shelton, ed., *As the Romans Did: A Sourcebook in Roman Social History.* New York: Oxford University Press, 1988, p. 345.
2. Quoted in Carlin A. Barton, *The Sorrow of the Ancient Romans: The Gladiator and the Monster.* Princeton: Princeton University Press, 1993, p. 12.
3. Juvenal, *Satires*, published as *Juvenal: The Sixteen Satires*, trans. Peter Green. New York: Penguin, 1974, p. 136.

Chapter Two: Training for a Dangerous Job

4. Plutarch, *Life of Crassus*, in *Parallel Lives*, excerpted in *Fall of the Roman Republic: Six Lives by Plutarch*, trans. Rex Warner. New York: Penguin, 1972, p. 122.

Chapter Three: The Fight to the Death

5. Quoted in Roland Auguet, *Cruelty and Civilization: The Roman Games.* London: Routledge, 1994, p. 80.
6. Martial, *Epigrams*, ed. and trans. D.R. Shackleton Bailey. 3 vols. Cambridge, MA: Harvard University Press, 1993, vol. 1, pp. 33, 35.

Chapter Four:
Chariot Races and Staged Naval Battles

7. Juvenal, *Satires,* p. 167.
8. Quoted in Shelton, *As the Romans Did,* p. 356.
9. Augustus, *Res gestae,* in Naphtali Lewis and Meyer Reinhold, eds., *Roman Civilization: Sourcebook II: The Empire.* New York: Harper and Row, 1966, p. 16.

Glossary

amphitheaters: Wooden or stone structures, usually oval-shaped and open at the top, in which the ancient Romans staged public games and shows, especially gladiatorial fights.

arena: The sandy area in the middle of an amphitheater or circus, where the performances took place.

circuses: Long wooden or stone structures in which the ancient Romans staged horse and chariot races. The most famous example was the Circus Maximus in Rome.

lanista: (plural, *lanistae*): professional supplier of gladiators.

ludi: (singular, *ludus*): A Gladiator school.

munus: (plural, *munera*): "Offering." A public show involving gladiators.

myrmillo: "Fish man." A kind of gladiator who carried a sword and rectangular shield.

naumachie: (singular, *naumachia*): Staged sea battles.

procurator: The owner or manager of a gladiator school.

retiarius: (plural, retiarii): "Net man." A kind of gladiator who wore no armor and carried a net and a long three-pronged spear.

For Further Exploration

Books

Phil R. Cox and Annabel Spenceley, *Who Were the Romans?* Boston: EDC, 1994. An impressive, well-illustrated introduction to the Romans, presented in a question-and-answer format.

John Malam, *Secret Worlds: Gladiators.* London: Dorling Kindersley, 2002. A beautifully illustrated book that brings the exciting but bloody gladiatorial combats of ancient Rome to life.

Anthony Marks and Graham Tingay, *The Romans.* London: Usborne, 1990. For basic readers, an excellent summary of the main aspects of Roman history, life, arts, and games, supported by hundreds of color drawings.

Don Nardo, *Roman Amphitheaters.* New York: Franklin Watts, 2002. Tells about the origins of the stone arenas where gladiators and animal hunters fought and often died and how these structures were built.

Judith Simpson, *Ancient Rome.* New York: Time-Life, 1997. A beautifully illustrated volume about ancient Roman civilization.

Richard Watkins, *Gladiator.* Boston: Houghton Mifflin, 1997. A very well-written, nicely illustrated overview of gladiators and their world for young readers.

Web Sites

The Circuses: Roman Chariot Racing (www.vroma. org/~bmcmanus/circus.html). Barbara F. McManus, College of New Rochelle. This is a well-written general overview of Roman chariot racing.

Ludus Gladiatorius (www.ludus.org.uk). Presented by an English reenactor group (modern people who stage authentic versions of gladiator fights), this site has many links to information about gladiatorial bouts, costumes, weapons, and tactics.

Roman Colosseum, Great Buildings Online (www. greatbuildings.com/buildings/Roman_Colosseum.html). A fine site about the great structure where many Roman spectacles took place. Has color pictures and a list of sources for further reading.

Index

Picture Credits

Cover, © Roger Wood/CORBIS
Art Renewal, 25
AKG-Images/Peter Connolly, 13, 22, 30
The Art Archive, 5, 10, 28, 37
Bridgeman Art Library, 9, 34-35
© Bettmann/CORBIS, 21
© Archivo Iconografico, S.A./CORBIS, 6
© Roger Wood/CORBIS, 24
© Gianni Berto Vanni/CORBIS, 15
© Pizzoli Alberto/CORBIS SYGMA, 19
© CORBIS, 18
Time-Life Pictures/Getty Images, 26-27
The Kobal Collection, 7, 16, 32-33, 36

About the Author

Historian Don Nardo has published many volumes about ancient Roman history and culture, including *The Punic Wars, The Age of Augustus, A Travel Guide to Ancient Rome, Life of a Roman Slave, The Greenhaven Encyclopedia of Greek and Roman Mythology,* and biographies of Julius Caesar and Cleopatra. Mr. Nardo also writes screenplays and teleplays and composes music. He lives in Massachusetts with his wife, Christine.

General Instruction
of the
Liturgy of the Hours

LITURGY DOCUMENTARY SERIES 5

United States Conference of Catholic Bishops • Washington, D.C.

Concordat cum originali:
   Msgr. James Patrick Moroney
   Executive Director, Secretariat for the Liturgy
   United States Conference of Catholic Bishops

In 2001 the National Conference of Catholic Bishops and United States Catholic Conference became the United States Conference of Catholic Bishops.

Cover image: Eyck, Jan van (c. 1390-1441). Singing angels, detail from the Ghent Altarpiece. Cathedral St. Bavo, Ghent, Belgium. Copyright © Scala/Art Resource, N.Y.

The English translation of the Decree, the Apostolic Constitution *Laudis Canticum*, and the General Instruction of the Liturgy of the Hours from *Documents on the Liturgy, 1963-1979: Conciliar, Papal and Curial Texts* © 1982, International Committee on English in the Liturgy, Inc. All rights reserved.

First printing, November 1983
Fourth printing, revised edition, December 2002

ISBN 1-57455-528-6

CONTENTS

GENERAL INSTRUCTION OF
THE LITURGY OF THE HOURS

Foreword

During a celebration of Morning Prayer at New York's Saint Patrick's Cathedral on 3 October 1979, Pope John Paul II stressed the importance of the Liturgy of the Hours in the life of the Church:

> The value of the Liturgy of the Hours is enormous. Through it all the faithful, but especially the clergy and religious, fulfill a role of prime importance: Christ's prayer goes on in the world. The Holy Spirit himself intercedes for God's people (see Rom 8:27). The Christian community, with praise and thanksgiving, glorifies the wisdom, the power, the providence, and the salvation of our God.

Through the Liturgy of the Hours or Divine Office, the Pope continued, "this prayer of Christ to which we give voice, our day is sanctified, our activities transformed, our actions made holy. We pray the same psalms that Jesus prayed and come into personal contact with him—the person to whom all Scripture points, the goal to which all history is directed" (John Paul II, Address at St. Patrick's Cathedral, New York City, 3 October 1979).

The purpose of this volume is to make better known the pastoral, theological, and liturgical introduction known as the General Instruction of the Liturgy of the Hours in a new official translation prepared by the International Commission on English in the Liturgy so that individuals, parishes, and other communities may gain a deeper appreciation of the importance of daily liturgical prayer.

The *editio typica* of the Liturgy of the Hours (*Liturgia Horarum*) was promulgated by Decree of the Congregation for Divine Worship on 11 April 1971 (Prot. N. 1000/71). The General Instruction of the Liturgy of the Hours, however, was issued separately in advance of the liturgical books by Decree of the same Congregation on 2 February 1971, while the Apostolic Constitution *Laudis Canticum* of Pope Paul VI promulgating both the General Instruction and the Liturgy of the Hours is dated 1 November 1970.

Before the translation of the *Liturgia Horarum* was completed by the International Commission on English in the Liturgy, the Federation of Diocesan Liturgical Commissions initiated and sponsored the preparation and publication of *The Prayer of Christians* or *American Interim Breviary*. Published in 1971, *The Prayer of Christians* followed the principles of the General Instruction of the Liturgy of the Hours and the structure and format of the hours of the soon-to-be published *Liturgia Horarum*. *The Prayer of Christians* served its purpose "ad interim" in acquainting American Catholics with the spirit and content of the new Office.

When ICEL completed the translation of the four-volume work *Liturgia Horarum* and presented it to the member conferences of bishops, the Bishops' Committee on the Liturgy submitted the Liturgy of the Hours to the National Conference of Catholic Bishops for its approval. A mail ballot was conducted in 1974 requesting approval of the English translation prepared by ICEL, the use of *The Grail Psalter* and of the English translations of the *Benedictus, Magnificat, Nunc Dimittis, Gloria Patri,* and *Te Deum* prepared by the International Consultation on Common Texts. The necessary majority was achieved, and on 21 October 1974 John Cardinal Krol, then president of the Conference, notified James Cardinal Knox, prefect of the Congregation for Divine Worship, of the *acta* of the Conference. Confirmation was received on 6 December 1974 (Prot. N. 2253/74). The official effective date was set by the Conference for 27 November 1977.

The complete four-volume edition of the Liturgy of the Hours was published by The Catholic Book Publishing Company, while the approved one-volume edition was published by The Liturgical Press, The Helicon Press, the Daughters of St. Paul, and The Catholic Book Publishing Company. Since 1977 excerpts from the Liturgy of the Hours, especially with musical settings, have been published. These latter editions have greatly helped many parishes, once unfamiliar with the Church's daily liturgical prayer, to begin to make the Liturgy of the Hours a regular part of parish life. The Bishops' Committee on the Liturgy hopes that this development will continue as Catholics increasingly discover the wealth of resources to be found in the Liturgy of the Hours.

Reverend John A. Gurrieri
Executive Director
Secretariat of the Bishops' Committee on the Liturgy
National Conference of Catholic Bishops

LIST OF ABBREVIATIONS

AA   Vatican Council II, *Apostolicam actuositatem* (Decree on the Apostolate of the Laity), 18 November 1965

AAS   *Acta Apostolicae Sedis: Commentarium Officiale* (Vatican City, 1909-)

AG   Vatican Council II, *Ad gentes* (Decree on the Church's Missionary Activity), 7 December 1965

CCL   *Corpus Christianorum, Series latina* (Turnhout, Belgium, 1953-)

CD   Vatican Council II, *Christus Dominus* (Decree on the Pastoral Office of Bishops in the Church), 28 October 1965

DV   Vatican Council II, *Dei verbum* (Dogmatic Constitution on Divine Revelation), 18 November 1965

GE   Vatican Council II, *Gravissimum educationis* (Declaration on Christian Education), 28 October 1965

GILH Sacred Congregation of Divine Worship, *Institutio Generalis de Liturga Horarum* (General Instruction of the Liturgy of the Hours), 2 February 1971

InterOec Sacred Congregation of Rites, instruction *Inter Oecumenici*, 26 September 1964

LG   Vatican Council II, *Lumen gentium* (Dogmatic Constitution on the Church), 21 November 1964

MusSacr Sacred Congregation of Rites, instruction *Musicam sacram*, 5 March 1967

OT   Vatican Council II, *Optatum totius* (Decree on Priestly Formation), 28 October 1965

PC   Vatican Council II, *Perfectae caritatis* (Decree on the Appropriate Renewal of the Religious Life), 28 October 1965

PG   Migne, J.-P. (ed.), *Patrologia graeca* (Paris, 1866-1884)

PL   Migne, J.-P. (ed.), *Patrologia latina* (Paris, 1844-1864)

PO   Vatican Council II, *Presbyterorum ordinis* (Decree on the Ministry and Life of Presbyters), 7 December 1965

RP   Roman Pontifical

SC   Vatican Council II, *Sacrosanctum Concilium* (Constitution on the Sacred Liturgy), 4 December 1963

SCR   Sacred Congregation of Rites

THE DIVINE OFFICE

Revised by Decree of the
Second Vatican Ecumenical Council
and Published by Authority of Pope Paul VI

THE LITURGY OF
THE HOURS

According to the Roman Rite

Approved by the Episcopal Conferences of
The Antilles, Bangladesh, Burma, Canada,
the Pacific CEPAC (Fiji Islands, Rarotonga, Samoa,
and Tokelau, Tonga), Ghana, India, New Zealand,
Pakistan, Papua New Guinea and The Solomons,
The Philippines, Rhodesia, South Africa, Sri Lanka,
Tanzania, Uganda, and the United States of America
for use in their dioceses
and confirmed by the Apostolic See

English translation prepared by the
International Committee on English in the Liturgy

SACRED CONGREGATION FOR DIVINE WORSHIP

DECREE

Prot. N. 1000/71

Through the liturgy of the hours, which from longstanding practice it celebrates throughout each day, the Church fulfills the Lord's command to pray without ceasing and at the same time offers praise to God the Father and intercedes for the salvation of the world.

Vatican Council II accordingly attached great importance to this established practice of the Church and intended its renewal. Therefore the Council took pains to ensure the proper reform of this manner of praying. Its intent was that priests and the other members of the Church might, in the present-day circumstances, carry out the office better and more completely (see SC art. 84).

This work of reform has been brought to its conclusion and approved by Pope Paul VI through the Apostolic Constitution *Laudis Canticum*, 1 November 1970. The Congregation for Divine Worship has therefore seen to the publication of the book composed in Latin for the celebration of the liturgy of the hours according to the Roman Rite. It declares the edition now being issued to be the *editio typica*.

Anything to the contrary notwithstanding.

From the office of the Congregation for Divine Worship, Easter Sunday, 11 April 1971.

✠ Arturo Cardinal Tabera
Prefect

Annibale Bugnini
Secretary

APOSTOLIC CONSTITUTION
The Divine Office
(*Laudis Canticum*)

PAUL, BISHOP
Servant of the Servants of God
For an Everlasting Memorial

T he hymn of praise that is sung through all the ages in the heavenly places and was brought by the High Priest, Christ Jesus, into this land of exile has been continued by the Church with constant fidelity over many centuries, in a rich variety of forms.

The liturgy of the hours gradually developed into the prayer of the local Church, a prayer offered at regular intervals and in appointed places under the presidency of a priest. It was seen as a kind of necessary complement by which the fullness of divine worship contained in the eucharistic sacrifice would overflow to reach all the hours of daily life.

The book of the divine office, gradually enlarged by many additions in the course of time, became a suitable instrument for the sacred service for which it was designed. Since over the generations a good many changes were introduced in the form of celebration, including the practice of individual recitation, it is not strange that the breviary, as it was sometimes called, underwent many transformations, sometimes affecting the principles of its arrangement.

The Council of Trent, unable, because of shortness of time, to complete the reform of the breviary, left this matter to the Apostolic See. The Roman Breviary, promulgated in 1568 by our predecessor St. Pius V, achieved above all what was so urgently needed, the introduction of uniformity in the canonical prayer of the Latin Church, after this uniformity had lapsed.

In subsequent centuries many revisions were made by Sixtus V, Clement VIII, Urban VIII, Clement XI, and other popes.

In 1911 St. Pius X promulgated a new breviary, prepared at his command. The ancient custom was restored of reciting the 150 psalms each week, and the arrangement of the psalter was entirely revised to remove all repetitions and to harmonize the weekday psalter and the cycle of biblical readings with the offices of saints. In addition, the office of Sunday was raised in rank and dignity to take general precedence over feasts of saints.

The whole work of liturgical revision was undertaken again by Pius XII. For both private and public recitation of the office he permitted the use of the new translation of the psalter prepared by the Pontifical Biblical Institute and in 1947 established a special commission with the responsibility of studying the question of the breviary. In 1955 all the bishops throughout the world were questioned about this matter. The fruits of this labor and concern were first seen in the decree on the simplification of the rubrics, published 23 March 1955, and in the regulations for the breviary issued by John XXIII in the *Codex rubricarum* of 1960.

Though only a part of the liturgical reform came under his seal, Pope John XXIII was aware that the fundamental principles on which the liturgy rests required further study. He entrusted this task to the Second Vatican Ecumenical Council, which in the meantime he had convoked. The result was that the Council treated the liturgy as a whole, and the hours in particular, with such thoroughness and skill, such spirituality and power, that there is scarcely a parallel to the Council's work in the entire history of the Church.

While Vatican Council II was still in session, it was our concern that after the promulgation of the Constitution on the Liturgy, its decrees should be put immediately into effect. For this purpose we established a special commission within the Consilium for the Implementation of the Constitution on the Liturgy. With the help of scholars and specialists in the liturgical, theological, spiritual, and pastoral disciplines, the Consilium worked with the greatest zeal and diligence over a period of seven years to produce the new book for the liturgy of the hours.

The principles underlying it, its whole arrangement, as well as its individual parts were approved by the Consilium and also by the 1967 Synod of Bishops, after consultation with the bishops of the whole Church and a very large number of pastors, religious, and laity.

It will be helpful here, then, to set out in detail the underlying principles and the structure of the liturgy of the hours.

1. As required by the Constitution *Sacrosanctum Concilium*, account was taken of the circumstances in which priests engaged in apostolic works find themselves today.

The office has been drawn up and arranged in such a way that not only clergy but also religious and indeed laity may participate in it, since it is the prayer of the whole people of God. People of different callings and circumstances, with their individual needs, were kept in mind, and a variety of ways of celebrating the office has been provided, by means of which the prayer can be adapted to suit the way of life and vocation of different groups dedicated to the liturgy of the hours.

2. Since the liturgy of the hours is the means of sanctifying the day, the order of this prayer was revised so that in the circumstances of contemporary life the canonical hours could be more easily related to the chronological hours of the day.

For this reason the hour of prime was suppressed; morning prayer and evening prayer, as hinges of the entire office, were assigned the most important role and now have the character of true morning and evening prayer; the office of readings retains its character as a night office for those who celebrate it during the night, but it is suitable for any hour of the day; the daytime prayer is so arranged that those who choose only one of the hours for midmorning, midday, and midafternoon may say the one most suitable to the actual time of day, without losing any part of the four-week psalter.

3. To ensure that in celebrating the office mind and voice may be more easily in harmony and that the liturgy of the hours may become in reality "a source of devotion and nourishment for personal prayer,"[1] in the new book, the amount of obligatory daily prayer has been considerably reduced, but variety in the texts has been notably increased and many aids to meditation on the psalms provided, for example, the captions, antiphons, psalm-prayers, and optional periods of silence.

4. In accordance with the ruling by the Council,[2] the weekly cycle of the psalter has been replaced by an arrangement of the psalms over a period of four weeks, in the new version prepared by the Commission for the Neo-Vulgate edition of the Bible, which we ourselves established. In this new arrangement of the psalms a few of the psalms and verses that are somewhat harsh in tone have been omitted, especially because of the difficulties anticipated from their use in vernacular celebration. In addition, new canticles from the Old Testament have been added to morning prayer in order to increase its spiritual richness, and canticles from the New Testament now enhance the beauty of evening prayer.

---

1   SC, art. 90.
2   SC, art. 91.

5. In the new cycle of readings from holy Scripture there is a more ample selection from the treasury of God's word, so planned as to harmonize with the cycle of readings at Mass.

The passages provide in general a certain unity of theme and have been chosen to present, in the course of the year, the principal stages in the history of salvation.

6. In accordance with the norms laid down by the Council, the daily reading from the works of the Fathers and of ecclesiastical writers has been revised in such a way that the best of the writings of Christian authors, especially of the Fathers, is included. Besides this, an optional lectionary will be prepared with a fuller selection from the spiritual riches of these writers, as a source of even more abundant benefits.

7. Anything that is not in harmony with historical truth has been removed from the text of the liturgy of the hours. On this score, the readings, especially biographies of the saints, have been revised in such a way that, first and foremost, the spiritual portrait of the saints and their significance for the life of the Church emerge and are placed in their true context.

8. Intercessions (*preces*) have been added to morning prayer to express the consecration of the day and to offer prayer for the day's work about to begin. There is also a short act of supplication at evening prayer, drawn up in the form of general intercessions.

The Lord's Prayer has been restored to its position at the end of these prayers. Since the Lord's Prayer is also said at Mass, this change represents a return in our time to early Christian usage, namely, of saying this prayer three times in the day.

Now that the prayer of holy Church has been reformed and entirely revised in keeping with its very ancient tradition and in the light of the needs of our day, it is to be hoped above all that the liturgy of the hours may pervade and penetrate the whole of Christian prayer, giving it life, direction, and expression and effectively nourishing the spiritual life of the people of God.

We have, therefore, every confidence that an appreciation of the prayer "without ceasing"[3] that our Lord Jesus Christ commanded will take on new life. The book for the liturgy of the hours, distributed as it is according to seasons, continually strengthens and supports that prayer. The very celebration of the liturgy of the hours, especially when a community gathered for this purpose expresses the genuine nature of the praying Church, stands as a wonderful sign of that Church.

Christian prayer above all is the prayer of the whole human community, which Christ joins to himself.[4] Everyone shares in this prayer, which is proper to the one Body as it offers prayers that give expression to the voice of Christ's beloved Bride, to the hopes and desires of the whole Christian people, and to supplications and petitions for the needs of all humanity.

This prayer takes its unity from the heart of Christ, for our Redeemer desired "that the life he had entered upon in his mortal body with supplications and with his sacrifice should continue without interruption through the ages in his Mystical Body, which is the Church."[5] Because of this, the prayer of the Church is at the same time "the very prayer that Christ himself, together with his Body, addresses to the Father."[6] As we celebrate the office, therefore, we must recognize our own voices echoing in Christ, his voice echoing in us.[7]

---

3   See Lk 18:1 and 21:36; 1 Thes 5:17; Eph 6:18.
4   See SC, art. 83.
5   Pius XII, Encycl. *Mediator Dei*, 20 Nov. 1947, no. 2: AAS 39 (1947) 522.
6   SC, art. 84.
7   See Augustine, *Enarrat. in Ps.* 85, 1: CCL 39, 1176.

To manifest this quality of our prayer more clearly, "the warm and living love for holy Scripture"[8] that permeates the liturgy of the hours must come to life in all of us, so that Scripture may indeed become the chief source of all Christian prayer. In particular, the praying of the psalms, which continually ponders and proclaims the action of God in the history of salvation, must be grasped with new warmth by the people of God. This will be achieved more readily if a deeper understanding of the psalms, in the meaning in which they are used in the liturgy, is more diligently promoted among the clergy and communicated to all the faithful by means of appropriate catechesis. The wider range of Scripture readings provided not only in the Mass but also in the new liturgy of the hours will enable the history of salvation to be constantly recalled and its continuation in the life of the human race to be effectively proclaimed.

The life of Christ in his Mystical Body also perfects and elevates the personal life of each member of the faithful. Any conflict therefore between the prayer of the Church and personal prayer must be entirely excluded; rather the relationship between them must be strengthened and enlarged. Mental prayer should draw unfailing nourishment from readings, psalms, and the other parts of the liturgy of the hours. The recitation of the office should be adapted, as far as possible, to the needs of living and personal prayer, so that as the General Instruction provides, rhythms and melodies are used and forms of celebration chosen that are more suited to the spiritual needs of those who pray it. If the prayer of the divine office becomes genuine personal prayer, the relation between the liturgy and the whole Christian life also becomes clearer. The whole life of the faithful, hour by hour during day and night, is a kind of *leitourgia* or public service, in which the faithful give themselves over to the ministry of love toward God and neighbor, identifying themselves with the action of Christ, who by his life and self-offering sanctified the life of all humanity.

---

8   SC, art. 24.

11

The liturgy of the hours clearly expresses and effectively strengthens this sublime truth, embodied in the Christian life.

For this reason the hours are recommended to all Christ's faithful members, including those who are not bound by law to their recitation.

Those who have received from the Church the mandate to celebrate the liturgy of the hours are to complete its entire course faithfully each day, respecting as far as possible the actual time of day; first and foremost, they are to give due importance to morning and evening prayer.

Those who are in holy orders and are marked in a special way with the sign of Christ the Priest, as well as those consecrated in a particular way to the service of God and of the Church by the vows of religious profession, should not only be moved to celebrate the hours through obedience to law, but should also feel themselves drawn to them because of the intrinsic excellence of the hours and their pastoral and ascetical value. It is extremely desirable that the public prayer of the Church be offered by all from hearts renewed, in acknowledgment of the inherent need within the whole Body of the Church: as the image of its Head, the Church must be described as the praying Church.

May the praise of God reecho in the Church of our day with greater grandeur and beauty by means of the new book for the liturgy of the hours, which now by Apostolic authority we sanction, approve, and promulgate. May it join the praise sung by saints and angels in the court of heaven. May it go from strength to strength in the days of this earthly exile and soon attain the fullness of praise that throughout eternity will be given "to the One who sits upon the throne and to the Lamb."[9]

---

9   Rev 5:13.

We decree that this new book for the liturgy of the hours may be put into use as soon as it is published. Meanwhile, the conferences of bishops are to see to the preparation of editions of this liturgical work in the vernacular and, after approval, that is, confirmation, of these editions by the Apostolic See, are to fix the date when the vernacular editions may or must be used, either in whole or in part. Beginning on the effective date for use of these versions in vernacular celebrations, only the revised form of the liturgy of the hours is to be followed, even by those who continue to use Latin.

For those however who, because of advanced age or for special reasons, experience serious difficulties in observing the new rite it is lawful to continue to use the former Roman Breviary, in whole or in part, with the consent of their Ordinary, and exclusively in individual recitation.

We wish that these decrees and prescriptions be firm and effective now and in the future, notwithstanding, to the extent necessary, apostolic constitutions and ordinances issued by our predecessors, and other prescriptions, even those deserving explicit mention and amendment.

PAUL VI

General Instruction of the Liturgy of the Hours

CHAPTER I
Importance of the Liturgy of the Hours or Divine Office in the Life of the Church

1. Public and common prayer by the people of God is rightly considered to be among the primary duties of the Church. From the very beginning those who were baptized "devoted themselves to the teaching of the apostles and to the community, to the breaking of the bread, and to prayer" (Acts 2:42). The Acts of the Apostles give frequent testimony to the fact that the Christian community prayed with one accord.[1]

The witness of the early Church teaches us that individual Christians devoted themselves to prayer at fixed times. Then, in different places, it soon became the established practice to assign special times for common prayer, for example, the last hour of the day when evening draws on and the lamp is lighted, or the first hour when night draws to a close with the rising of the sun.

In the course of time other hours came to be sanctified by prayer in common. These were seen by the Fathers as foreshadowed in the Acts of the Apostles. There we read of the disciples gathered together at the third hour.[2] The prince of the apostles "went up on the housetop to pray, about the sixth hour" (10:9); "Peter and John were going up to

---

1   See Acts 1:14, 4:24, 12:5 and 12. See also Eph 5:19-21.
2   See Acts 2:1-15.

the temple at the hour of prayer, the ninth hour" (3:1); "about midnight Paul and Silas were praying and singing hymns to God" (16:25).

2. Such prayer in common gradually took the form of a set cycle of hours. This liturgy of the hours or divine office, enriched by readings, is principally a prayer of praise and petition. Indeed, it is the prayer of the Church with Christ and to Christ.

I. PRAYER OF CHRIST
Christ the Intercessor with the Father
3. When the Word, proceeding from the Father as the splendor of his glory, came to give us all a share in God's life, "Christ Jesus, High Priest of the new and eternal covenant, taking human nature, introduced into this earthly exile the hymn of praise that is sung throughout all ages in the halls of heaven."[3] From then on in Christ's heart the praise of God assumes a human sound in words of adoration, expiation, and intercession, presented to the Father by the Head of the new humanity, the Mediator between God and his people, in the name of all and for the good of all.

4. In his goodness the Son of God, who is one with his Father (see Jn 10:30) and who on entering the world said, "Here I am! I come, God, to do your will" (Heb 10:9; see Jn 6:38), has left us the lesson of his own prayer. The Gospels many times show us Christ at prayer: when his mission is revealed by the Father;[4] before he calls the apostles;[5] when he blesses God at the multiplication of the loaves;[6] when he is transfigured on the mountain;[7] when he heals the deaf-mute;[8] when he

---

3   SC, art. 83.
4   See Lk 3:21-22.
5   See Lk 6:12.
6   See Mt 14:19, 15:36; Mk 6:41, 8:7; Lk 9:16; Jn 6:11.
7   See Lk 9:28-29.
8   See Mk 7:34.

raises Lazarus;[9] before he asks for Peter's confession of faith;[10] when he teaches the disciples how to pray;[11] when the disciples return from their mission;[12] when he blesses the little children;[13] when he prays for Peter.[14]

The work of each day was closely bound up with his prayer, indeed flowed out from it: he would retire into the desert or into the hills to pray,[15] rise very early,[16] or spend the night up to the fourth watch[17] in prayer to God.[18]

We are right in thinking that he took part both in public prayers—in the synagogues, which he entered on the Sabbath "as his custom was;"[19] in the temple, which he called a house of prayer[20]—and in the private prayers that for devout Israelites were a daily practice. He used the traditional blessings of God at meals, as is expressly mentioned in connection with the multiplication of the loaves,[21] the last supper,[22] and the meal at Emmaus.[23] He also joined with the disciples in a hymn of praise.[24]

---

9   See Jn 11:41ff.

10   See Lk 9:18.

11   See Lk 11:1.

12   See Mt 11:25ff; Lk 10:21ff.

13   See Mt 19:13.

14   See Lk 22:32.

15   See Mk 1:35, 6:46; Lk 5:16. See also Mt 4:1 and par.; Mt 14:23.

16   See Mk 1:35.

17   See Mt 14:23 and 25; Mk 6:46 and 48.

18   See Lk 6:12.

19   See Lk 4:16.

20   See Mt 21:13 and par.

21   See Mt 14:19 and par.; Mt 15:36 and par.

22   See Mt 26:26 and par.

23   See Lk 24:30.

24   See Mt 26:30 and par.

To the very end of his life, as his passion was approaching,[25] at the last supper,[26] in the agony in the garden,[27] and on the cross,[28] the divine teacher showed that prayer was the soul of his Messianic ministry and paschal death. "In the days of his life on earth he offered up prayers and entreaties with loud cries and tears to the one who could deliver him from death and because of his reverence his prayer was heard" (Heb 5:7). By a single offering on the altar of the cross "he has made perfect forever those who are being sanctified" (Heb 10–14). Raised from the dead, he lives for ever, making intercession for us.[29]

II. PRAYER OF THE CHURCH
Commandment to Pray

5. Jesus has commanded us to do as he did. On many occasions he said: "Pray," "ask," "seek"[30] "in my name."[31] He taught us how to pray in what is known as the Lord's Prayer.[32] He taught us that prayer is necessary,[33] that it should be humble,[34] watchful,[35] persevering, confident in the Father's goodness,[36] single-minded, and in conformity with God's nature.[37]

Here and there in their letters the apostles have handed on to us many prayers, particularly of praise and thanks. They instruct us on prayer

---

25 See Jn 12:27ff.

26 See Jn 17:1-26.

27 See Mt 26:36-44 and par.

28 See Lk 23:34 and 46; Mt 27:46; Mk 15:34.

29 See Heb 7:25.

30 Mt 5:44, 7:7, 26:41; Mk 13:33, 14:38; Lk 6:28, 10:2, 11:9, 22:40 and 46.

31 Jn 14:13ff, 15:16, 16:23ff, and 26.

32 See Mt 6:9-13; Lk 11:2-4.

33 See Lk 18:1.

34 See Lk 18:9-14.

35 See Lk 21:36; Mk 13:33.

36 See Lk 11:5-13, 18:1-8; Jn 14:13, 16:23.

37 See Mt 6:5-8, 23:14; Lk 20:47; Jn 4:23.

in the Holy Spirit,[38] through Christ,[39] offered to God,[40] as to its persistence and constancy,[41] its power to sanctify,[42] and on prayer of praise,[43] thanks,[44] petition,[45] and intercession for all.[46]

Christ's Prayer Continued by the Church

6. Since we are entirely dependent on God, we must acknowledge and express this sovereignty of the Creator, as the devout people of every age have done by means of prayer.

Prayer directed to God must be linked with Christ, the Lord of all, the one Mediator[47] through whom alone we have access to God.[48] He unites to himself the whole human community[49] in such a way that there is an intimate bond between the prayer of Christ and the prayer of all humanity. In Christ and in Christ alone human worship of God receives its redemptive value and attains its goal.

7. There is a special and very close bond between Christ and those whom he makes members of his Body, the Church, through the sacrament of rebirth. Thus, from the Head all the riches belonging to the Son flow throughout the whole Body: the communication of the Spirit, the truth, the life, and the participation in the divine sonship that Christ manifested in all his prayer when he dwelt among us.

---

38   See Rom 8:15 and 26; 1 Cor 12:3; Gal 4:6; Jude 20.

39   See 2 Cor 1:20; Col 3:17.

40   See Heb 13:15.

41   See Rom 12:12; 1 Cor 7:5; Eph 6:18; Col 4:2; 1 Thes 5:17; 1 Tm 5:5; 1 Pt 4:7.

42   See 1 Tm 4:5; Jas 5:1ff; 1 Jn 3:22, 5:14ff.

43   See Eph 5:19ff; Heb 13:15; Rev 19:5.

44   See Col 3:17; Phil 4:6; 1 Thes 5:17; 1 Tm 2:1.

45   See Rom 8:26; Phil 4:6.

46   See Rom 15:30; 1 Tm 2:1ff; Eph 6:18; 1 Thes 5:25; Jas 5:14 and 16.

47   See 1 Tm 2:5; Heb 8:6, 9:15, 12:24.

48   See Rom 5:2; Eph 2:18, 3:12.

49   See SC, art. 83.

Christ's priesthood is also shared by the whole Body of the Church, so that the baptized are consecrated as a spiritual temple and holy priesthood through the rebirth of baptism and the anointing by the Holy Spirit[50] and are empowered to offer the worship of the New Covenant, a worship that derives not from our own powers but from Christ's merit and gift.

God could give us no greater gift than to establish as our Head the Word through whom he created all things and to unite us to that Head as members. The results are many. The Head is Son of God and Son of Man, one as God with the Father and one as man with us. When we speak in prayer to the Father, we do not separate the Son from him; and when the Son's Body prays, it does not separate itself from its Head. It is the one Savior of his Body, the Lord Christ Jesus, who prays for us and in us and who is prayed to by us. He prays for us as our priest, in us as our Head; he is prayed to by us as our God. Recognize therefore our own voice in him and his voice in us.[51]

The excellence of Christian prayer lies in its sharing in the reverent love of the only-begotten Son for the Father and in the prayer that the Son put into words in his earthly life and that still continues without ceasing in the name of the whole human race and for its salvation, throughout the universal Church and in all its members.

Action of the Holy Spirit
8. The unity of the Church at prayer is brought about by the Holy Spirit, who is the same in Christ,[52] in the whole Church, and in every

---

50   See LG, no. 10.

51   Augustine, *Enarrat. in Ps.* 85, 1: CCL 39, 1176.

52   See Lk 10:21, the occasion when Jesus "rejoiced in the Holy Spirit and said: 'I thank you, Father. . . .'"

baptized person. It is this Spirit who "helps us in our weakness" and "intercedes for us with longings too deep for words" (Rom 8:26). As the Spirit of the Son, he gives us "the spirit of adopted children, by which we cry out: Abba, Father" (Rom 8:15; see Gal 4:6; 1 Cor 12:3; Eph 5:18; Jude 20). There can be therefore no Christian prayer without the action of the Holy Spirit, who unites the whole Church and leads it through the Son to the Father.

Community Character of Prayer

9. It follows that the example and precept of our Lord and the apostles in regard to constant and persevering prayer are not to be seen as a purely legal regulation. They belong to the very essence of the Church itself, which is a community and which in prayer must express its nature as a community. Hence, when the community of believers is first mentioned in the Acts of the Apostles, it is seen as a community gathered together at prayer "with the women and Mary, the mother of Jesus, and his brothers" (Acts 1:14). "There was one heart and soul in the company of those who believed" (Acts 4:32). Their oneness in spirit was founded on the word of God, on the communion of charity, on prayer, and on the eucharist.[53]

Though prayer in private and in seclusion[54] is always necessary and to be encouraged[55] and is practiced by the members of the Church through Christ in the Holy Spirit, there is a special excellence in the prayer of the community. Christ himself has said: "Where two or three are gathered together in my name, I am there in their midst" (Mt 18:20).

---

53 See Acts 2:42 Gr.

54 See Mt 6:6.

55 See SC, art. 12.

III. LITURGY OF THE HOURS

Consecration of Time

10. Christ taught us: "You must pray at all times and not lose heart" (Lk 18:1). The Church has been faithful in obeying this instruction; it never ceases to offer prayer and makes this exhortation its own: "Through him [Jesus] let us offer to God an unceasing sacrifice of praise" (Heb 15:15). The Church fulfills this precept not only by celebrating the eucharist but in other ways also, especially through the liturgy of the hours. By ancient Christian tradition what distinguishes the liturgy of the hours from other liturgical services is that it consecrates to God the whole cycle of the day and the night.[56]

11. The purpose of the liturgy of the hours is to sanctify the day and the whole range of human activity. Therefore its structure has been revised in such a way as to make each hour once more correspond as nearly as possible to natural time and to take account of the circumstances of life today.[57]

Hence, "that the day may be truly sanctified and the hours themselves recited with spiritual advantage, it is best that each of them be prayed at a time most closely corresponding to the true time of each canonical hour."[58]

Liturgy of the Hours and the Eucharist

12. To the different hours of the day the liturgy of the hours extends[59] the praise and thanksgiving, the memorial of the mysteries of salvation, the petitions and the foretaste of heavenly glory that are present in the eucharistic mystery, "the center and high point in the whole life of the Christian community."[60]

---

56   See SC, art. 83-84.
57   See SC, art. 88.
58   SC, art. 94.
59   See PO, no. 5.
60   CD, no. 30.

The liturgy of the hours is in turn an excellent preparation for the celebration of the eucharist itself, for it inspires and deepens in a fitting way the dispositions necessary for the fruitful celebration of the eucharist: faith, hope, love, devotion, and the spirit of self-denial.

Priesthood of Christ in the Liturgy of the Hours

13. In the Holy Spirit Christ carries out through the Church "the task of redeeming humanity and giving perfect Glory to God,"[61] not only when the eucharist is celebrated and the sacraments administered but also in other ways and especially when the liturgy of the hours is celebrated.[62] There Christ himself is present—in the gathered community, in the proclamation of God's word, "in the prayer and song of the Church."[63]

Sanctification of God's People

14. Our sanctification is accomplished[64] and worship is offered to God in the liturgy of the hours in such a way that an exchange or dialogue is set up between God and us, in which "God is speaking to his people . . . and his people are responding to him by both song and prayer."[65]

Those taking part in the liturgy of the hours have access to holiness of the richest kind through the life-giving word of God, which in this liturgy receives great emphasis. Thus its readings are drawn from sacred Scripture, God's words in the psalms are sung in his presence, and the intercessions, prayers, and hymns are inspired by Scripture and steeped in its spirit.[66]

Hence, not only when those things are read "that are written for our instruction" (Rom 15:4), but also when the Church prays or sings,

---

61   SC, art. 5.

62   See SC, art. 83 and 98.

63   SC, art. 7.

64   See SC, art. 10.

65   SC, art. 33.

66   See SC, art. 24.

faith is deepened for those who take part and their minds are lifted up to God, in order to offer him their worship as intelligent beings and to receive his grace more plentifully.[67]

Praising God with the Church in Heaven

15. In the liturgy of the hours the Church exercises the priestly office of its Head and offers to God "without ceasing"[68] a sacrifice of praise, that is, a tribute of lips acknowledging his name.[69] This prayer is "the voice of a bride addressing her bridegroom; it is the very prayer that Christ himself, together with his Body, addresses to the Father."[70] "All who render this service are not only fulfilling a duty of the Church, but also are sharing in the greatest honor of Christ's Bride for by offering these praises to God they are standing before God's throne in the name of the Church, their Mother."[71]

16. When the Church offers praise to God in the liturgy of the hours, it unites itself with that hymn of praise sung throughout all ages in the halls of heaven;[72] it also receives a foretaste of the song of praise in heaven, described by John in the Book of Revelation, the song sung continually before the throne of God and of the Lamb. Our close union with the Church in heaven is given effective voice "when we all, from every tribe and tongue and people and nation redeemed by Christ's blood (see Rev 5:9) and gathered together into the one Church, glorify the triune God with one hymn of praise."[73]

The prophets came almost to a vision of this liturgy of heaven as the victory of a day without night, of a light without darkness: "The sun

---

67 See SC, art. 33.
68 1 Thes 5:17.
69 See Heb 13:15.
70 SC, art. 84.
71 SC, art. 85.
72 See SC, art. 83.
73 LG, no. 50; SC, art. 8 and 104.

will no more be your light by day, and the brightness of the moon will not shine upon you, but the Lord will be your everlasting light" (Is 60:19; see Rv 21:23 and 25). "There will be a single day, known to the Lord, not day and night, and at evening there will be light" (Zech 14:7). Already "the end of the ages has come upon us (see 1 Cor 10:11) and the renewal of the world has been irrevocably established and in a true sense is being anticipated in this world."[74] By faith we too are taught the meaning of our temporal life, so that we look forward with all creation to the revealing of God's children.[75] In the liturgy of the hours we proclaim this faith, we express and nourish this hope, we share in some degree the joy of everlasting praise and of that day that knows no setting.

Petition and Intercession

17. But besides the praise of God, the Church in the liturgy of the hours expresses the prayers and desires of all the faithful; indeed, it prays to Christ, and through him to the Father, for the salvation of the whole world.[76] The Church's voice is not just its own; it is also Christ's voice, since its prayers are offered in Christ's name, that is, "through our Lord Jesus Christ," and so the Church continues to offer the prayer and petition that Christ poured out in the days of his earthly life[77] and that have therefore a unique effectiveness. The ecclesial community thus exercises a truly maternal function in bringing souls to Christ, not only by charity, good example, and works of penance but also by prayer.[78]

The concern with prayer involves those especially who have been called by a special mandate to carry out the liturgy of the hours: bishops and

---

74   LG, no. 48.

75   See Rom 8:19.

76   See SC, art. 83.

77   See Heb 5:7.

78   See PO, no. 6.

priests as they pray in virtue of their office for their own people and for the whole people of God;[79] other sacred ministers; and also religious.[80]

18. Those then who take part in the liturgy of the hours bring growth to God's people in a hidden but fruitful apostolate,[81] for the work of the apostolate is directed to this end, "that all who are made children of God by faith and baptism should come together to praise God in the midst of this Church, to take part in the sacrifice, and to eat the Lord's Supper."[82]

Thus by their lives the faithful show forth and reveal to others "the mystery of Christ and the real nature of the true Church. It is of the essence of the Church to be visible yet endowed with invisible resources, eager to act yet intent on contemplation, present in this world yet not at home in it."[83]

In their turn the readings and prayers of the liturgy of the hours form a wellspring of the Christian life: the table of sacred Scripture and the writings of the saints nurture its life and prayers strengthen it. Only the Lord, without whom we can do nothing,[84] can, in response to our request, give power and increase to what we do,[85] so that we may be built up each day in the Spirit into the temple of God,[86] to the measure of Christ's fullness,[87] and receive greater strength also to bring the good news of Christ to those outside.[88]

---

79   See LG, no. 41.
80   See no. 24 of this Instruction.
81   See PC, no. 7.
82   SC, art. 10.
83   SC, art. 2.
84   See Jn 15:5.
85   See SC, art. 86.
86   See Eph 2:21-22.
87   See Eph 4:13.
88   See SC, art. 2.

Harmony of Mind and Voice

19. Mind and voice must be in harmony in a celebration that is worthy, attentive, and devout, if this prayer is to be made their own by those taking part and to be a source of devotion, a means of gaining God's manifold grace, a deepening of personal prayer, and an incentive to the work of the apostolate.[89] All should be intent on cooperating with God's grace, so as not to receive it in vain. Seeking Christ, penetrating ever more deeply into his mystery through prayer,[90] they should offer praise and petition to God with the same mind and heart as the divine Redeemer when he prayed.[R1]

---

89   See SC, art. 90. *Rule of St. Benedict,* ch. 19.

90   See PO, no. 14; OT, no. 8.

R1   Query: When a person recites the liturgy of the hours, do the readings have to be pronounced or simply read? Reply: *It is enough simply to read them.* The conciliar Constitution on the Liturgy says nothing about an obligation to oral recitation when a person says the office alone, although there was a difference of opinion on this among the conciliar Fathers. They decreed a reform of the breviary not for the purpose of shortening the time for prayer but of giving all who celebrate the liturgy of the hours a better time for prayer. Accordingly, all the documents treating of the reform of the divine office urge that "the mind be attuned to the voice" and that "the prayer of the Church be a source of devotion and nourishment also for personal prayer" (SC, art. 90). This calls for the reading of Scripture and the Fathers as well as the recitation of the psalms, in which God is speaking to his people and they are responding (see SC, art. 33), to consist "not in a cursory reading of a breviary" (see Schema of SC, *Modi a Patribus Conciliaribus propositi, a Commissione de sacra Liturgia examinati* vol. 4, *De Officio Divino,* 13) but in personal meditation. Otherwise even if there is a recitation of the hours, there is no penetration by the word of God nor true prayer. The true course is "that as we celebrate the office, we must recognize our own voices echoing in Christ, his voice echoing in us" (Paul VI, Ap. Const. *Laudis canticum*). This is the way for the liturgy of the hours to be a personal prayer, sincere and effective, a source of devotion, the sustenance of the spiritual life and of each day's apostolic labors. Then the relationship between the Church's prayer and personal prayer is strengthened and mental prayer has an unfailing source in the readings, the psalms, and other parts of the liturgy of the hours (see ibid.). Sometimes a surer guarantee for this objective of the liturgy of the hours in individual recitation may be to omit the oral recitation of each word, especially in the case of the readings: Not 9 (1973) 150.

IV. PARTICIPANTS IN THE LITURGY OF THE HOURS
A. Celebration in Common

20. The liturgy of the hours, like other liturgical services, is not a private matter but belongs to the whole Body of the Church, whose life it both expresses and affects.[91] This liturgy stands out most strikingly as an ecclesial celebration when, through the bishop surrounded by his priests and ministers,[92] the local Church celebrates it. For "in the local Church the one, holy, catholic, and apostolic Church is truly present and at work."[93] Such a celebration is therefore most earnestly recommended.

When, in the absence of the bishop, a chapter of canons or other priests celebrate the liturgy of the hours, they should always respect the true time of day and, as far as possible, the people should take part. The same is to be said of collegiate chapters.

21. Wherever possible, other groups of the faithful should celebrate the liturgy of the hours communally in church. This especially applies to parishes—the cells of the diocese, established under their pastors, taking the place of the bishop; they "represent in some degree the visible Church established throughout the world."[94]

22. Hence, when the people are invited to the liturgy of the hours and come together in unity of heart and voice, they show forth the Church in its celebration of the mystery of Christ.[95]

23. Those in holy orders or with a special canonical mission[96] have the responsibility of initiating and directing the prayer of the community;

---

91   See SC, art. 26.
92   See SC, art. 41.
93   CD, no. 11.
94   See art. 42. See also AA, no. 10.
95   See SC, art. 26 and 84.
96   See AG, no. 17.

"they should expend every effort so that those entrusted to their care may become of one mind in prayer."[97] They must therefore see to it that the people are invited, and prepared by suitable instruction, to celebrate the principal hours in common, especially on Sundays and holydays.[98] They should teach the people how to make this participation a source of genuine prayer;[99] they should therefore give the people suitable guidance in the Christian understanding of the psalms, in order to progress by degrees to a greater appreciation and more frequent use of the prayer of the Church.[100]

24. Communities of canons, monks, nuns, and other religious who celebrate the liturgy of the hours by rule or according to their constitutions, whether with the general rite or a particular rite, in whole or in part, represent in a special way the Church at prayer. They are a fuller sign of the Church as it continuously praises God with one voice and they fulfill the duty of "working," above all by prayer, "to build up and increase the whole Mystical Body of Christ, and for the good of the local Churches."[101] This is especially true of those living the contemplative life.

25. Even when having no obligation to communal celebration, all sacred ministers and all clerics living in a community or meeting together should arrange to say at least some part of the liturgy of the hours in common, particularly morning prayer and evening prayer.[102]

26. Men and women religious not bound to a common celebration, as well as members of any institute of perfection, are strongly urged to gather together, by themselves or with the people, to celebrate the liturgy of the hours or part of it.

---

97   CD, no. 15.
98   See SC, art. 100.
99   See PO, no. 5.
100   See nos. 100-109 of this Instruction.
101   CD, no. 33; see also PC, nos. 6, 7, 15; AG, no. 15.
102   See SC, art. 99.

27. Lay groups gathering for prayer, apostolic work, or any other reason are encouraged to fulfill the Church's duty[103] by celebrating part of the liturgy of the hours. The laity must learn above all how in the liturgy they are adoring God the Father in spirit and in truth;[104] they should bear in mind that through public worship and prayer they reach all humanity and can contribute significantly to the salvation of the whole world.[105]

Finally, it is of great advantage for the family, the domestic sanctuary of the Church, not only to pray together to God but also to celebrate some parts of the liturgy of the hours as occasion offers, in order to enter more deeply into the life of the Church.[106]

B. Mandate to Celebrate the Liturgy of the Hours

28. Sacred ministers have the liturgy of the hours entrusted to them in such a particular way that even when the faithful are not present they are to pray it themselves with the adaptations necessary under these circumstances. The Church commissions them to celebrate the liturgy of the hours so as to ensure at least in their persons the regular carrying out of the duty of the whole community and the unceasing continuance of Christ's prayer in the Church.[107]

The bishop represents Christ in an eminent and conspicuous way and is the high priest of his flock; the life in Christ of his faithful people may be said in a sense to derive from him and depend on him.[108] He should, then, be the first of all the members of his Church in offering prayer. His prayer in the recitation of the liturgy of the hours is always made in the name of the Church and on behalf of the Church entrusted to him.[109]

---

103   See SC, art. 100.
104   See Jn 4:23.
105   See GE, no. 2; AA, no. 16.
106   See AA, no. 11.
107   See PO, no. 13.
108   See SC, art. 41; LG, no. 21.
109   See LG, no. 26; CD, no. 15.

United as they are with the bishop and the whole presbyterium, priests are themselves representative in a special way of Christ the Priest[110] and so share the same responsibility of praying to God for the people entrusted to them and indeed for the whole world.[111]

All these ministers fulfill the ministry of the Good Shepherd who prays for his sheep that they may have life and so be brought into perfect unity.[112] In the liturgy of the hours that the Church sets before them they are not only to find a source of devotion and a strengthening of personal prayer,[113] but must also nourish and foster pastoral mission-ary activity as the fruit of their contemplation to gladden the whole Church of God.[114]

29. Hence bishops, priests, and deacons aspiring to the priesthood, who have received from the Church the mandate to celebrate the liturgy of the hours (see no. 17), are bound by the obligation of reciting the full sequence of hours each day,[114b] observing as far as possible the true time of day.

They should, first and foremost, attach due importance to those hours that are, so to speak, the two hinges of the liturgy of the hours, that is, morning prayer and evening prayer, which should not be omitted except for a serious reason.

They should faithfully pray the office of readings, which is above all a liturgical celebration of the word of God. In this way they fulfill daily a

---

110   See PO, no. 13.
111   See PO, no. 5.
112   See Jn 10:11, 17:20 and 23.
113   See SC, art. 90.
114   See LG, no. 41.
114b   *Code of Canon Law*, can. 276 §2, 3 and can. 1174 §1.

duty that is peculiarly their own, that is, of receiving the word of God into their lives, so that they may become more perfect as disciples of the Lord and experience more deeply the unfathomable riches of Christ.[115]

In order to sanctify the whole day more completely, they will also treasure the recitation of daytime prayer and night prayer, to round off the whole *Opus Dei* and to commend themselves to God before retiring.

30. Permanent deacons, to whom the mandate of the Church also applies, are to recite daily the part of the liturgy of the hours that has been determined by the conference of bishops.[116]

31. a. Cathedral and collegiate chapters should celebrate in choir those parts of the liturgy of the hours that are prescribed for them by the general law or by particular law.

In private recitation individual members of these chapters should include those hours that are recited in their chapter,[R2] in addition to the hours prescribed for all sacred ministers.[117]

---

115 See DV, no. 25; PO, no. 13.

116 See *Code of Canon Law*, can. 276 §2, 3. Paul VI, Motu Proprio *Sacrum Diaconatus Ordinem*, 18 June 1967, no. 27: AAS 59 (1967), 703.

R2 Query: What should the arrangement be in celebrating the liturgy of the hours in cathedral chapters? Reply: The GILH, nos. 76 and 31, regulate the celebration of the liturgy of the hours in chapters of canons: "[Text quoted, nos. 76 and 31]." Particular law is to determine in detail which hours must be celebrated by the chapter; the individual members who are absent from the capitular celebration must recite such hours privately. The greatest care is to be taken to celebrate the hours at the corresponding natural time of day, with solemnity and the participation of the people. There is to be no combining of more than one hour at the same celebration. Now that the GILH has been published, it is required that the practice of chapters be made to conform to it. If necessary there is to be a revision of the capitular statutes and approval by the authority competent to give it. The aim is that the service to the liturgy rendered by the chapter reflect the documents of the liturgical reform: Not. 8 (1972) 192.

117 See SCR, Instr. InterOec, no. 78b.

b. Religious communities bound to the recitation of the liturgy of the hours and their individual members should celebrate the hours in keeping with their own particular law; but the prescription of no. 29 in regard to those in holy orders is to be respected.

Communities bound to choir should celebrate the whole sequence of the hours daily in choir;[118] when absent from choir their members should recite the hours in keeping with their own particular law; but the prescriptions in no. 29 are always to be respected.

32. Other religious communities and their individual members are advised to celebrate some parts of the liturgy of the hours, in accordance with their own situation, for it is the prayer of the Church that makes the whole Church, scattered throughout the world, one in heart and mind.[119]

This recommendation applies also to laypersons.[120]

C. Structure of the Celebration

33. The structure of the liturgy of the hours follows laws of its own and incorporates in its own way elements found in other Christian celebrations. Thus it is so constructed that, after a hymn, there is always psalmody, then a long or short reading of sacred Scripture, and finally prayer of petition.

In a celebration in common and in private recitation the essential structure of this liturgy remains the same, that is, it is a conversation between God and his people. Celebration in common, however, expresses more clearly the ecclesial nature of the liturgy of the hours; it makes for active participation by all, in a way suited to each one's condition, through the

---

118   See SC, art. 95.

119   See Acts 4:32.

120   See SC, art. 100.

acclamations, dialogue, alternating psalmody, and similar elements. It also better provides for the different literary genres that make up the liturgy of the hours.[121] Hence, whenever it is possible to have a celebration in common, with the people present and actively taking part, this kind of celebration is to be preferred to one that is individual and, as it were, private.[122] It is also advantageous to sing the office in choir and in community as opportunity offers, in accordance with the nature and function of the individual parts.

In this way the Apostle's exhortation is obeyed: "Let the word of Christ dwell in you in all its fullness, as you teach and counsel each other in all wisdom by psalms, hymns, and spiritual canticles, singing thankfully to God in your hearts" (Col 3:16; see Eph 5:19-20).

---

121   See SC, art. 26, 28-30.
122   See SC, art. 27.

CHAPTER II
Sanctification of the Day:
The Different Liturgical Hours

I. INTRODUCTION TO THE WHOLE OFFICE

34. The whole office begins as a rule with an invitatory. This consists in the verse, *Lord, open my lips. And my mouth will proclaim your praise*, and Ps 95. This psalm invites the faithful each day to sing God's praise and to listen to his voice and draws them to hope for "the Lord's rest."[1]

In place of Ps 95, Ps 100, Ps 67, or Ps 24 may be used as circumstances may suggest.

It is preferable to recite the invitatory psalm responsorially as it is set out in the text, that is, with the antiphon recited at the beginning, then repeated, and repeated again after each strophe.

35. The invitatory is placed at the beginning of the whole sequence of the day's prayer, that is, it precedes either morning prayer or the office of readings, whichever of these liturgical rites begins the day. The invitatory psalm with its antiphon may be omitted, however, when the invitatory is the prelude to morning prayer.

36. The variation of the invitatory antiphon, to suit the different liturgical days, is indicated at its place of occurrence.

---

1   See Heb 3:7–4:16.

II. MORNING PRAYER AND EVENING PRAYER

37. "By the venerable tradition of the universal Church, lauds as morning prayer and vespers as evening prayer are the two hinges on which the daily office turns; hence they are to be considered as the chief hours and celebrated as such."[2]

38. As is clear from many of the elements that make it up, morning prayer is intended and arranged to sanctify the morning. St. Basil the Great gives an excellent description of this character in these words:

> It is said in the morning in order that the first stirrings of our mind and will may be consecrated to God and that we may take nothing in hand until we have been gladdened by the thought of God, as it is written: 'I was mindful of God and was glad' (Ps 77:4 [Jerome's translation from Hebrew]), or set our bodies to any task before we do what has been said: 'I will pray to you, Lord, you will hear my voice in the morning; I will stand before you in the morning and gaze on you' (Ps 5:4-5).[3]

Celebrated as it is as the light of a new day is dawning, this hour also recalls the resurrection of the Lord Jesus, the true light enlightening all people (see Jn 1:9) and "the sun of justice" (Mal 4:2), "rising from on high" (Lk 1:78). Hence, we can well understand the advice of St. Cyprian: "There should be prayer in the morning so that the resurrection of the Lord may thus be celebrated."[4]

39. When evening approaches and the day is already far spent, evening prayer is celebrated in order that "we may give thanks for what has been given us, or what we have done well, during the day."[5] We also

---

2 SC, art. 89a; see also art. 100.
3 Basil the Great, *Regulae fusius tractatae* resp. 37, 3: PG 31, 1014.
4 Cyprian, *De oratione dominica* 35: PL 4, 561.
5 Basil the Great, *Regulae fusius tractatae* resp. 37, 3: PG 31, 1015.

recall the redemption through the prayer we send up "like incense in the Lord's sight," and in which "the raising up of our hands" becomes "an evening sacrifice."[6] This sacrifice "may also be interpreted more spiritually as the true evening sacrifice that our Savior the Lord entrusted to the apostles at supper on the evening when he instituted the sacred mysteries of the Church or of the evening sacrifice of the next day, the sacrifice, that is, which, raising his hands, he offered to the Father at the end of the ages for the salvation of the whole world."[7] Again, in order to fix our hope on the light that knows no setting, "we pray and make petition for the light to come down on us anew; we implore the coming of Christ who will bring the grace of eternal light."[8] Finally, at this hour we join with the Churches of the East in calling upon the "joy-giving light of that holy glory, born of the immortal, heavenly Father, the holy and blessed Jesus Christ; now that we have come to the setting of the sun and have seen the evening star, we sing in praise of God, Father, Son, and Holy Spirit. . . ."

40. Morning prayer and evening prayer are therefore to be accorded the highest importance as the prayer of the Christian community. Their public or communal celebration should be encouraged, especially in the case of those who live in community. Indeed, the recitation of these hours should be recommended also to individual members of the faithful unable to take part in a celebration in common.

41. Morning prayer and evening prayer begin with the introductory verse, *God, come to my assistance. Lord, make haste to help me.* There follows the *Glory to the Father*, with *As it was in the beginning* and *Alleluia* (omitted in Lent). This introduction is omitted at morning prayer when the invitatory immediately precedes it.

---

6   See Ps 141:2.

7   John Cassian, *De institutione coenob.* 3, 3: PL 49, 124, 125.

8   Cyprian, *De oratione dominica* 35: PL 4, 560.

42. Then an appropriate hymn is sung immediately. The purpose of the hymn is to set the tone for the hour or the feast and, especially in celebrations with a congregation, to form a simple and pleasant introduction to prayer.

43. After the hymn the psalmody follows, in accordance with the rules laid down in nos. 121-125. The psalmody of morning prayer consists of one morning psalm, then a canticle from the Old Testament and, finally, a second psalm of praise, following the tradition of the Church.

The psalmody of evening prayer consists of two psalms (or two parts of a longer psalm) suited to the hour and to celebration with a congregation and a canticle from the letters of the apostles or from the Book of Revelation.

44. After the psalmody there is either a short reading or a longer one.

45. The short reading is provided to fit the day, the season, and the feast. It is to be read and received as a true proclamation of God's word that emphasizes some holy thought or highlights some shorter passages that may be overlooked in the continuous cycle of Scripture readings.

The short readings are different for each day of the psalter cycle.

46. Especially in a celebration with a congregation, a longer Scripture reading may be chosen either from the office of readings or the Lectionary for Mass, particularly texts that for some reason have not been used. From time to time some other more suitable reading may be used, in accordance with the rules in nos. 248-249 and 251.

47. In a celebration with a congregation a short homily may follow the reading to explain its meaning, as circumstances suggest.

48. After the reading or homily a period of silence may be observed.

49. As a response to the word of God, a responsorial chant or short responsory is provided; this may be omitted. Other chants with the same purpose and character may also be substituted in its place, provided these have been duly approved by the conference of bishops.

50. Next is the solemn recitation of the gospel canticle with its antiphon, that is, the Canticle of Zechariah at morning prayer and the Canticle of Mary at evening prayer. Sanctioned by age-old popular usage in the Roman Church, these canticles are expressions of praise and thanksgiving for our redemption. The antiphon for each canticle is indicated, according to the character of the day, the season, or the feast.

51. After the canticle, at morning prayer come the petitions for the consecration of the day and its work to God and at evening prayer, the intercessions (see nos. 179-193).

52. After the petitions or intercessions the Lord's Prayer is said by all.

53. Immediately after the Lord's Prayer there follows the concluding prayer, which for weekdays in Ordinary Time is found in the psalter and for other days in the proper.

54. Then, if a priest or deacon is presiding, he dismisses the congregation with the greeting, *The Lord be with you*, and the blessing as at Mass.

He adds the invitation, *Go in peace*. R̶/. *Thanks be to God*. In the absence of a priest or deacon the celebration concludes with *May the Lord bless us*, etc.

III. OFFICE OF READINGS

55. The office of readings seeks to provide God's people, and in particular those consecrated to God in a special way, with a wider selection of passages from sacred Scripture for meditation, together with the finest excerpts from spiritual writers. Even though the cycle of

scriptural readings at daily Mass is now richer, the treasures of revelation and tradition to be found in the office of readings will also contribute greatly to the spiritual life. Bishops and priests in particular should prize these treasures, so that they may hand on to others the word of God they have themselves received and make their teaching "the true nourishment for the people of God."[9]

56. But prayer should accompany "the reading of sacred Scripture so that there may be a conversation between God and his people: 'we talk with God when we pray, we listen to him when we read God's words.'"[10] For this reason the office of readings consists also of psalms, a hymn, a prayer, and other texts, giving it the character of true prayer.

57. The Constitution on the Liturgy directs that the office of readings, "though it should retain its character as a night office of praise when celebrated in choir, shall be adapted so that it may be recited at any hour of the day; it shall be made up of fewer psalms and longer readings."[11]

58. Those who are obliged by their own particular law and others who commendably wish to retain the character of this office as a night office of praise (either by saying it at night or very early in the morning and before morning prayer) during Ordinary Time choose the hymn from the selection given for this purpose. Moreover, for Sundays, solemnities, and certain feasts what is said in nos. 70-73 about vigils must be kept in mind.

59. Without prejudice to the regulations just given, the office of readings may be recited at any hour of the day, even during the night hours of the previous day, after evening prayer has been said.

---

9   RP, Ordination of Priests, no. 14.

10   Ambrose, *De officiis ministrorum* 1, 20, 88: PL 16, 50. See also DV, no. 25.

11   SC, art. 89c.

60. If the office of readings is said before morning prayer, the invitatory precedes it, as noted (nos. 34-36). Otherwise it begins with the verse, *God, come to my assistance* with the *Glory to the Father, As it was in the beginning*, and the *Alleluia* (omitted in Lent).

61. Then the hymn is sung. In Ordinary Time this is taken either from the night selections, as already indicated (nos. 34-36), or from the morning selections, depending on what the true time of day requires.

62. The psalmody follows and consists of three psalms (or parts in the case of longer psalms). During the Easter triduum, on days within the octaves of Easter and Christmas, on solemnities and feasts, the psalms are proper, with their proper antiphons.

On Sundays and weekdays, however, the psalms and their antiphons are taken from the current week and day of the psalter. On memorials of the saints they are similarly taken from the current week and day of the psalter, unless there are proper psalms or antiphons (see nos. 218ff).

63. Between the psalmody and the readings there is, as a rule, a verse, marking a transition in the prayer from psalmody to listening.

64. There are two readings: the first is from the Scriptures, the second is from the writings of the Fathers or church writers, or else is a reading connected with the saints.

65. After each reading there is a responsory (see nos. 169-172).

66. The scriptural reading is normally to be taken from the Proper of Seasons, in accordance with the rules to be given later (nos. 140-155). On solemnities and feasts, however, it is taken from the proper or the common.

67. On solemnities and feasts of saints a proper second reading is used; if there is none, the second reading is taken from the respective

Common of Saints. On memorials of saints when the celebration is not impeded, the reading in connection with the saint replaces the current second reading (see nos. 166 and 235).

68. On Sundays outside Lent, on days within the octaves of Easter and Christmas, and on solemnities and feasts the *Te Deum* is said after the second reading with its responsory but is omitted on memorials and weekdays. The last part of this hymn, that is, from the verse, *Save your people, Lord* to the end, may be omitted.

69. The office of readings normally concludes with the prayer proper to the day and, at least in recitation in common, with the acclamation, *Let us praise the Lord. R/. And give him thanks.*

IV. VIGILS

70. The Easter Vigil is celebrated by the whole Church, in the rites given in the relevant liturgical books. "The vigil of this night," as St. Augustine said, "is of such importance that it could claim exclusively for itself the name 'vigil,' common though this is to all the others."[12] "We keep vigil on that night when the Lord rose again and inaugurated for us in his humanity that life . . . in which there is neither death nor sleep. . . . Hence, the one whose resurrection we celebrate by keeping watch a little longer will see to it that we reign with him by living a life without end."[13]

71. As with the Easter Vigil, it was customary to begin certain solemnities (different in different Churches) with a vigil. Among these solemnities Christmas and Pentecost are preeminent. This custom should be maintained and fostered, according to the particular usage of each Church. Whenever it seems good to add a vigil for other solemnities or pilgrimages, the general norms for celebrations of the word should be followed.

---

12   Augustine, *Sermo Guelferbytanus* 5: PL Suppl 2, 550.
13   Ibid.: PL Suppl 2, 552.

72. The Fathers and spiritual writers have frequently encouraged Christians, especially those who lead the contemplative life, to pray during the night. Such prayer expresses and awakens our expectation of the Lord's Second Coming: "At midnight the cry went up: 'See, the bridegroom is coming, go out to meet him'" (Mt 25:6). "Keep watch, then, for you do not know when the master of the house is coming, whether late or at midnight or at cockcrow or in the morning, so that if he comes unexpectedly he may not find you sleeping" (Mk 13:35-36). All who maintain the character of the office of readings as a night office, therefore, are to be commended.

73. Further, since in the Roman Rite the office of readings is always of a uniform brevity, especially for the sake of those engaged in apostolic work, those who desire, in accordance with tradition, to extend the celebration of the vigils of Sundays, solemnities, and feasts should do so as follows.

First, the office of readings is to be celebrated as in *The Liturgy of the Hours* up to the end of the readings. After the two readings and before the *Te Deum* canticles should be added from the special appendix of *The Liturgy of the Hours*. Then the gospel should be read; a homily on the gospel may be added. After this the *Te Deum* is sung and the prayer said.

On solemnities and feasts the gospel is to be taken from the Lectionary for Mass; on Sundays, from the series on the paschal mystery in the appendix of *The Liturgy of the Hours*.

V. DAYTIME HOURS

74. Following a very ancient tradition Christians have made a practice of praying out of private devotion at various times of the day, even in the course of their work, in imitation of the Church in apostolic times. In different ways with the passage of time this tradition has taken the form of a liturgical celebration.

75. Liturgical custom in both East and West has retained midmorning, midday, and midafternoon prayer, mainly because these hours were linked to a commemoration of the events of the Lord's passion and of the first preaching of the Gospel.

76. Vatican Council II decreed that these lesser hours are to be retained in choir.[14]

The liturgical practice of saying these three hours is to be retained, without prejudice to particular law, by those who live the contemplative life. It is recommended also for all, especially those who take part in retreats or pastoral meetings.

77. Outside choir, without prejudice to particular law, it is permitted to choose from the three hours the one most appropriate to the time of day, so that the tradition of prayer in the course of the day's work may be maintained.

78. Daytime prayer is so arranged as to take into account both those who recite only one hour and those who are obliged, or desire, to say all three hours.

79. The daytime hours begin with the introductory verse, *God, come to my assistance* with the *Glory to the Father, As it was in the beginning,* and the *Alleluia* (omitted in Lent). Then a hymn appropriate to the hour is sung. The psalmody is next, then the reading, followed by the verse. The hour concludes with the prayer and, at least in recitation in common, with the acclamation, *Let us praise the Lord.* ℟. *And give him thanks.*

80. Different hymns and prayers are given for each of the hours so that, in keeping with tradition, they may correspond to the true time of day

---

14   See SC, art. 89.

and thus sanctify it in a more pointed way. Those who recite only one hour should therefore choose the texts that correspond to the true time of day.

In addition the readings and prayers vary in keeping with the character of the day, the season, or the feast.

81. Two psalmodies are provided; the current psalmody and the complementary psalmody. Those who pray one hour should use the current psalmody. Those who pray more than one hour should use the current psalmody at one hour and the complementary psalmody at the others.

82. The current psalmody consists of three psalms (or parts in the case of longer psalms) from the psalter, with their antiphons, unless directions are given to the contrary.

On solemnities, the Easter triduum, and days within the octave of Easter, proper antiphons are said with three psalms chosen from the complementary psalmody, unless special psalms are to be used or the celebration falls on a Sunday, when the psalms are those from the Sunday of Week I of the psalter.

83. The complementary psalter consists of three sets of three psalms, chosen as a rule from the Gradual Psalms.

VI. NIGHT PRAYER

84. Night prayer is the last prayer of the day, said before retiring, even if that is after midnight.

85. Night prayer begins like the other hours, with the verse, *God, come to my assistance,* the *Glory to the Father, As it was in the beginning,* and the *Alleluia* (omitted in Lent).

86. It is a laudable practice to have next an examination of conscience; in a celebration in common this takes place in silence or as part of a penitential rite based on the formularies in the Roman Missal.

87. The appropriate hymn follows.

88. After evening prayer I of Sunday the psalmody consists of Ps 4 and Ps 134; after evening prayer II of Sunday it consists of Ps 91.

On the other days psalms are chosen that are full of confidence in the Lord; it is permissible to use the Sunday psalms instead, especially for the convenience of those who may wish to pray night prayer from memory.

89. After the psalmody there is a reading, followed by the responsory, *Into your hands*. Then, as a climax to the whole hour, the Canticle of Simeon, *Lord, now you let your servant go in peace* follows, with its antiphon.

90. The concluding prayer then follows, as it appears in the psalter.

91. After the prayer the blessing, *May the all-powerful Lord* is used, even in private recitation.

92. Finally, one of the antiphons in honor of the Blessed Virgin Mary is said. In the Easter season this is always to be the *Regina caeli*. In addition to the antiphons given in *The Liturgy of the Hours*, others may be approved by the conferences of bishops.[15]

VII. COMBINING THE HOURS WITH MASS OR WITH EACH OTHER

93. In particular cases, if circumstances require, it is possible to link an hour more closely with Mass when there is a celebration of the liturgy

---

15   See SC, art. 38.

of the hours in public or in common, according to the norms that follow, provided the Mass and the hour belong to one and the same
office. Care must be taken, however, that this does not result in harm
to pastoral work, especially on Sundays.

94. When morning prayer, celebrated in choir or in common, comes
immediately before Mass, the whole celebration may begin either with
the introductory verse and hymn of morning prayer, especially on
weekdays, or with the entrance song, procession, and celebrant's greeting, especially on Sundays and holy days; one of the introductory rites
is thus omitted.

The psalmody of morning prayer follows as usual, up to, but
excluding, the reading. After the psalmody the penitential rite is omitted
and, as circumstances suggest, the *Kyrie*; the *Gloria* then follows, if
required by the rubrics, and the celebrant says the opening prayer of
the Mass. The liturgy of the word follows as usual.

The general intercessions are made in the place and form customary at
Mass. But on weekdays, at Mass in the morning, the intercessions of
morning prayer may replace the daily form of the general intercessions
at Mass.

After the communion with its communion song the Canticle of
Zechariah, *Blessed be the Lord*, with its antiphon from morning prayer,
is sung. Then follow the prayer after communion and the rest as usual.

95. If public celebration of a daytime hour, whichever corresponds to
the time of day, is immediately followed by Mass, the whole celebration may begin in the same way, either with the introductory verse and
hymn for the hour, especially on weekdays, or with the entrance song,
procession, and celebrant's greeting, especially on Sundays and holy
days; one of the introductory rites is thus omitted.

The psalmody of the hour follows as usual up to, but excluding, the reading. After the psalmody the penitential rite is omitted and, as circumstances suggest, the *Kyrie*; the *Gloria* then follows, if required by the rubrics and the celebrant says the opening prayer of the Mass.

96. Evening prayer, celebrated immediately before Mass, is joined to it in the same way as morning prayer. Evening prayer I of solemnities, Sundays, or feasts of the Lord falling on Sundays may not be celebrated until after Mass of the preceding day or Saturday.

97. When a daytime hour or evening prayer follows Mass, the Mass is celebrated in the usual way up to and including the prayer after communion.

When the prayer after communion has been said, the psalmody of the hour begins without introduction. At the daytime hour, after the psalmody the short reading is omitted and the prayer is said at once and the dismissal takes place as at Mass. At evening prayer, after the psalmody the short reading is omitted and the Canticle of Mary with its antiphon follows at once; the intercessions and the Lord's Prayer are omitted; the concluding prayer follows, then the blessing of the congregation.

98. Apart from Christmas eve, the combining of Mass with the office of readings is normally excluded, since the Mass already has its own cycle of readings, to be kept distinct from any other. But if by way of exception, it should be necessary to join the two, then immediately after the second reading from the office, with its responsory, the rest is omitted and the Mass begins with the *Gloria*, if it is called for; otherwise the Mass begins with the opening prayer.

99. If the office of readings comes immediately before another hour of the office, then the appropriate hymn for that hour may be sung at the beginning of the office of readings. At the end of the office of readings the prayer and conclusion are omitted, and in the following hour the introductory verse with the *Glory to the Father* is omitted.

CHAPTER III
Different Elements in the Liturgy of the Hours

I. PSALMS AND THEIR CONNECTION WITH CHRISTIAN PRAYER

100. In the liturgy of the hours the Church in large measure prays through the magnificent songs that the Old Testament authors composed under the inspiration of the Holy Spirit. The origin of these verses gives them great power to raise the mind to God, to inspire devotion, to evoke gratitude in times of favor, and to bring consolation and courage in times of trial.

101. The psalms, however, are only a foreshadowing of the fullness of time that came to pass in Christ the Lord and that is the source of the power of the Church's prayer. Hence, while the Christian people are all agreed on the supreme value to be placed on the psalms, they can sometimes experience difficulty in making this inspired poetry their own prayer.

102. Yet the Holy Spirit, under whose inspiration the psalms were written, is always present by his grace to those believers who use them with good will. But more is necessary: the faithful must "improve their understanding of the Bible, especially of the psalms,"[1] according to their individual capacity, so that they may understand how and by what method they can truly pray through the psalms.

---

1   SC, art. 90.

103. The psalms are not readings or prose prayers, but poems of praise. They can on occasion be recited as readings, but from their literary genre they are properly called *Tehillim* ("songs of praise") in Hebrew and *psalmoi* ("songs to be sung to the lyre") in Greek. In fact, all the psalms have a musical quality that determines their correct style of delivery. Thus even when a psalm is recited and not sung or is said silently in private, its musical character should govern its use. A psalm does present a text to the minds of the people, but its aim is to move the heart of those singing it or listening to it and also of those accompanying it "on the lyre and harp."

104. To sing the psalms with understanding, then, is to meditate on them verse by verse, with the heart always ready to respond in the way the Holy Spirit desires. The one who inspired the psalmist will also be present to those who in faith and love are ready to receive his grace. For this reason the singing of psalms, though it demands the reverence owed to God's majesty, should be the expression of a joyful spirit and a loving heart, in keeping with their character as sacred poetry and divine song and above all with the freedom of the children of God.

105. Often the words of a psalm help us to pray with greater ease and fervor, whether in thanksgiving and joyful praise of God or in prayer for help in the throes of suffering. But difficulties may arise, especially when the psalm is not addressed directly to God. The psalmist is a poet and often addresses the people as he recalls Israel's history; sometimes he addresses others, including subrational creatures. He even represents the words as being spoken by God himself and individual people, including, as in Ps 2, God's enemies. This shows that a psalm is a different kind of prayer from a prayer or collect composed by the Church. Moreover, it is in keeping with the poetic and musical character of the psalms that they do not necessarily address God but are sung in God's presence. Thus St. Benedict's instruction: "Let us reflect on what it

means to be in the sight of God and his angels, and let us so stand in his presence that our minds are in harmony with our voices."[2]

106. In praying the psalms we should open our hearts to the different attitudes they express, varying with the literary genre to which each belongs (psalms of grief, trust, gratitude, etc.) and to which biblical scholars rightly attach great importance.

107. Staying close to the meaning of the words, the person who prays the psalms looks for the significance of the text for the human life of the believer.

It is clear that each psalm was written in its own individual circumstances, which the titles given for each psalm in the Hebrew psalter are meant to indicate. But whatever its historical origin, each psalm has its own meaning, which we cannot overlook even in our own day. Though the psalms originated very many centuries ago among an Eastern people, they express accurately the pain and hope, the unhappiness and trust of people of every age and country, and sing above all of faith in God, of revelation, and of redemption.

108. Those who pray the psalms in the liturgy of the hours do so not so much in their own name as in the name of the entire Body of Christ. This consideration does away with the problem of a possible discrepancy between personal feelings and the sentiments a psalm is expressing: for example, when a person feels sad and the psalm is one of joy or when a person feels happy and the psalm is one of mourning. Such a problem is readily solved in private prayer, which allows for the choice of a psalm suited to personal feelings. The divine office, however, is not private; the cycle of psalms is public, in the name of the Church, even for those who may be reciting an hour alone. Those who pray the psalms in the name of the Church nevertheless can always find

---

2   *Rule of St. Benedict,* ch. 19.

a reason for joy or sadness, for the saying of the Apostle applies in this case also: "Rejoice with the joyful and weep with those who weep" (Rom 12:15). In this way human frailty, wounded by self-love, is healed in proportion to the love that makes the heart match the voice that prays the psalms.[3]

109. Those who pray the psalms in the name of the Church should be aware of their full sense (*sensus plenus*), especially their Messianic sense, which was the reason for the Church's introduction of the psalter into its prayer. This Messianic sense was fully revealed in the New Testament and indeed was affirmed publicly by Christ the Lord in person when he said to the apostles: "All that is written about me in the law of Moses and the prophets and the psalms must be fulfilled" (Lk 24:44). The best-known example of this Messianic sense is the dialogue in Matthew's Gospel on the Messiah as Son of David and David's Lord,[4] where Ps 110 is interpreted as Messianic.

Following this line of thought, the Fathers of the Church saw the whole psalter as a prophecy of Christ and the Church and explained it in this sense; for the same reason the psalms have been chosen for use in the liturgy. Though somewhat contrived interpretations were at times proposed, in general the Fathers, and the liturgy itself had the right to hear in the singing of the psalms the voice of Christ crying out to the Father or of the Father conversing with the Son; indeed, they also recognized in the psalms the voice of the Church, the apostles, and the martyrs. This method of interpretation also flourished in the Middle Ages; in many manuscripts of the period the Christological meaning of each psalm was set before those praying by means of the caption prefixed. A Christological meaning is by no means confined to the recognized Messianic psalms but is given also to many others. Some of these interpretations are doubtless Christological only in an accommodated sense, but they have the support of the Church's tradition.

---

3   See *Rule of St. Benedict,* ch. 19.

4   See Mt 22:44ff.

On the great feasts especially, the choice of psalms is often based on their Christological meaning and antiphons taken from these psalms are frequently used to throw light on this meaning.

II. ANTIPHONS AND OTHER AIDS TO PRAYING THE PSALMS
110. In the Latin tradition of psalmody three elements have greatly contributed to an understanding of the psalms and their use as Christian prayer: the captions, the psalm-prayers, and in particular the antiphons.

111. In the psalter of *The Liturgy of the Hours* a caption is given for each psalm to explain its meaning and its import for the personal life of the believer. These captions are intended only as an aid to prayer. A quotation from the New Testament or the Fathers of the Church is added to foster prayer in the light of Christ's new revelation; it is an invitation to pray the psalms in their Christological meaning.

112. Psalm-prayers for each psalm are given in the supplement to *The Liturgy of the Hours* as an aid to understanding them in a predominantly Christian way. An ancient tradition provides a model for their use: after the psalm a period of silence is observed, then the prayer gives a resumé and resolution of the thoughts and aspirations of those praying the psalms.

113. Even when the liturgy of the hours is recited, not sung, each psalm retains its own antiphon, which is also to be said in private recitation. The antiphons help to bring out the literary genre of the psalm; they highlight some theme that may otherwise not attract the attention it deserves; they suggest an individual tone in a psalm, varying with different contexts: indeed, as long as farfetched accommodated senses are avoided, antiphons are of great value in helping toward an understanding of the typological meaning or the meaning appropriate to the feast; they can also add pleasure and variety to the recitation of the psalms.

114. The antiphons in the psalter have been designed to lend themselves to vernacular translation and to repetition after each strophe, in

accordance with no. 125. When the office of Ordinary Time is recited, not sung, the quotations printed with the psalms may be used in place of these antiphons (see no. 111).

115. When a psalm may be divided because of its length into several sections within one and the same hour, an antiphon is given for each section. This is to provide variety, especially when the hour is sung, and also to help toward a better understanding of the riches of the psalm. Still, it is permissible to say or sing the complete psalm without interruption, using only the first antiphon.

116. Proper antiphons are given for each of the psalms of morning prayer and evening prayer during the Easter triduum, on the days within the octaves of Easter and Christmas, on the Sundays of the seasons of Advent, Christmas, Lent, and Easter, on the weekdays of Holy Week and the Easter season, and from 17 to 24 December.

117. On solemnities proper antiphons are given for the office of readings, morning prayer, the daytime hours, and evening prayer; if not, the antiphons are taken from the common. On feasts the same applies to the office of readings and to morning prayer and evening prayer.

118. Any memorials of the saints that have proper antiphons retain them (see no. 235).

119. The antiphons for the Canticles of Zechariah and of Mary are taken, during Ordinary Time, from the Proper of Seasons, if they are given there; if not, they are taken from the current week and day of the psalter. On solemnities and feasts they are taken from the proper if they are given there; if not, they are taken from the common. On memorials without proper antiphons the antiphon may be taken at will either from the common or from the current week.

120. During the Easter season *Alleluia* is added to all antiphons, unless it would clash with the meaning of a particular antiphon.

III. WAYS OF SINGING THE PSALMS

121. Different psalms may be sung in different ways for a fuller grasp of their spiritual meaning and beauty. The choice of ways is dictated by the literary genre or length of each psalm, by the language used, whether Latin or the vernacular, and especially by the kind of celebration, whether individual, with a group, or with a congregation. The reason for using psalms is not the establishment of a fixed amount of prayer but their own variety and the character proper to each.

122. The psalms are sung or said in one of three ways, according to the different usages established in tradition or experience: directly (*in directum*), that is, all sing the entire psalm; or antiphonally, that is, two choirs or sections of the congregation sing alternate verses or strophes; or responsorially.

123. At the beginning of each psalm its own antiphon is always to be recited. as noted in nos. 113-120. At the end of the psalm the practice of concluding with the *Glory to the Father* and *As it was in the beginning* is retained. This is the fitting conclusion endorsed by tradition and it gives to Old Testament prayer a note of praise and a Christological and Trinitarian sense. The antiphon may be repeated at the end of the psalm.

124. When longer psalms occur, sections are marked in the psalter that divide the parts in such a way as to keep the threefold structure of the hour; but great care has been taken not to distort the meaning of the psalm.

It is useful to observe this division, especially in a choral celebration in Latin; the *Glory to the Father* is added at the end of each section.

It is permissible, however, either to keep this traditional way or to pause between the different sections of the same psalm or to recite the whole psalm and its antiphon as a single unit without a break.

125. In addition, when the literary genre of a psalm suggests it, the divisions into strophes are marked in order that, especially when the psalm is sung in the vernacular, the antiphons may be repeated after each strophe; in this case the *Glory to the Father* need be said only at the end of the psalms.

IV. PLAN FOR THE DISTRIBUTION OF
THE PSALMS IN THE OFFICE

126. The psalms are distributed over a four-week cycle in such a way that very few psalms are omitted, while some, traditionally more important, occur more frequently than others; morning prayer and evening prayer as well as night prayer have been assigned to psalms appropriate to these hours.[5]

127. Since morning prayer and evening prayer are particularly designed for celebration with a congregation, the psalms chosen for them are those more suited to this purpose.

128. For night prayer the norm given in no. 88 has been followed.

129. For Sunday, including its office of readings and daytime prayer, the psalms chosen are those that tradition has particularly singled out as expressions of the paschal mystery. Certain psalms of a penitential character or connected with the passion are assigned to Friday.

130. Three psalms (78, 105, and 106) are reserved for the seasons of Advent, Christmas, Lent, and Easter, because they throw a special light on the Old Testament history of salvation as the forerunner of its fulfillment in the New.

131. Three psalms (58, 83, and 109) have been omitted from the psalter cycle because of their curses; in the same way, some verses have been

---

5   See SC, art. 91.

omitted from certain psalms, as noted at the head of each. The reason for the omission is a certain psychological difficulty, even though the psalms of imprecation are in fact used as prayer in the New Testament, for example, Rv 6:10, and in no sense to encourage the use of curses.

132. Psalms too long to be included in one hour of the office are assigned to the same hour on different days so that they may be recited in full by those who do not usually say other hours. Thus Ps 119 is divided in keeping with its own internal structure and is spread over twenty-two days during daytime prayer, because tradition has assigned it to the day hours.

133. The four-week cycle of the psalter is coordinated with the liturgical year in such a way that on the First Sunday of Advent, the First Sunday in Ordinary Time, the First Sunday of Lent, and Easter Sunday the cycle is always begun again with Week I (others being omitted when necessary).

After Pentecost, when the psalter cycle follows the series of weeks in Ordinary Time, it begins with the week indicated in the Proper of Seasons at the beginning of the appropriate week in Ordinary Time.

134. On solemnities and feasts, during the Easter triduum, and on the days within the octaves of Easter and Christmas, proper psalms are assigned to the office of readings from those with a tradition of use at these times and their relevance is generally highlighted by the choice of antiphon. This is also the case at daytime prayer on certain solemnities of the Lord and during the octave of Easter. At morning prayer the psalms and canticle are taken from the Sunday of the Week I of the psalter. On solemnities the psalms at evening prayer I are taken from the *Laudate* Psalms, following an ancient custom. At evening prayer II on solemnities and at evening prayer on feasts the psalms and canticle are proper. At daytime prayer on solemnities (except those already mentioned and those falling on Sunday) the psalms are taken from the

Gradual Psalms; at daytime prayer on feasts the psalms are those of the current week and day of the psalter.

135. In all other cases the psalms are taken from the current week and day of the psalter, unless there are proper antiphons or proper psalms.

V. CANTICLES FROM THE OLD AND NEW TESTAMENTS

136. At morning prayer between the first and the second psalm a canticle from the Old Testament is inserted, in accordance with custom. In addition to the series handed down from the ancient Roman tradition and the other series introduced into the breviary by St. Pius X, several other canticles have been added to the psalter from different books of the Old Testament, in order that each weekday of the four-week cycle may have its own proper canticle and on Sunday the two sections of the Canticle of the Three Children may be alternated.

137. At evening prayer, after the two psalms, a canticle of the New Testament is inserted, from the letters of the apostles or the Book of Revelation. Seven canticles are given for each week of the four-week cycle, one for each day. On the Sundays of Lent, however, in place of the *Alleluia* Canticle from the Book of Revelation, the canticle is from the First Letter of Peter. In addition, on the solemnity of the Epiphany and the feast of the Transfiguration the canticle is from the First Letter to Timothy; this is indicated in those offices.

138. The gospel Canticles of Zechariah, of Mary, and of Simeon are to be treated with the same solemnity and dignity as are customary at the proclamation of the gospel itself.

139. Both psalmody and readings are arranged in keeping with the received rule of tradition that the Old Testament is read first, then the writings of the apostles, and finally the gospel.

VI. READINGS FROM SACRED SCRIPTURE
A. Reading of Sacred Scripture in General

140. The reading of sacred Scripture, which, following an ancient tradition, takes place publicly in the liturgy, is to have special importance for all Christians, not only in the celebration of the eucharist but also in the divine office. The reason is that this reading is not the result of individual choice or devotion but is the planned decision of the Church itself, in order that in the course of the year the Bride of Christ may unfold the mystery of Christ "from his incarnation and birth until his ascension, the day of Pentecost, and the expectation of blessed hope and of the Lord's return."[6] In addition, the reading of sacred Scripture in the liturgical celebration is always accompanied by prayer in order that the reading may have greater effect and that, in turn, prayer—especially the praying of the psalms—may gain fuller understanding and become more fervent and devout because of the reading.

141. In the liturgy of the hours there is a longer reading of sacred Scripture and a shorter reading.

142. The longer reading, optional at morning prayer and evening prayer, is described in no. 46.

B. Cycle of Scripture Readings in the Office of Readings

143. The cycle of readings from sacred Scripture in the office of readings takes into account both those special seasons during which by an ancient tradition particular books are to be read and the cycle of readings at Mass. The liturgy of the hours is thus coordinated with the Mass in such a way that the scriptural readings in the office complement the readings at Mass and so provide a complete view of the history of salvation.

---

6   SC, art. 102.

144. Without prejudice to the exception noted in no. 73, there are no readings from the Gospel in the liturgy of the hours, since in the Mass each year the Gospel is read in its entirety.

145. There are two cycles of biblical readings. The first is a one-year cycle and is incorporated into *The Liturgy of the Hours*; the second, given in the supplement for optional use, is a two-year cycle, like the cycle of readings at weekday Masses in Ordinary Time.

146. The two-year cycle of readings for the liturgy of the hours is so arranged that each year there are readings from nearly all the books of sacred Scripture as well as longer and more difficult texts that are not suitable for inclusion in the Mass. The New Testament as a whole is read each year, partly in the Mass, partly in the liturgy of the hours; but for the Old Testament books a selection has been made of those parts that are of greater importance for the understanding of the history of salvation and for deepening devotion.

The complementarity between the readings in the liturgy of the hours and in the Mass in no way assigns the same texts to the same days or spreads the same books over the same seasons. This would leave the liturgy of the hours with the less important passages and upset the sequence of texts. Rather this complementarity necessarily demands that the same book be used in the Mass and in the liturgy of the hours in alternate years or that, if it is read in the same year, there be some interval in between.

147. During Advent, following an ancient tradition, passages are read from Isaiah in a semicontinuous sequence, alternating in a two-year cycle. In addition, the Book of Ruth and certain prophecies from Micah are read. Since there are special readings from 17 to 24 December (both dates included), readings for the Third Week of Advent which fall on these dates are omitted.

148. From 29 December until 5 January the readings for Year I are taken from the Letter to the Colossians (which considers the incarnation of the Lord within the context of the whole history of salvation), and the readings for Year II are taken from the Song of Songs (which foreshadows the union of God and humanity in Christ): "God the Father prepared a wedding feast for God his Son when he united him with human nature in the womb of the Virgin, when he who is God before all ages willed that his Son should become man at the end of the ages."[7]

149. From 7 January until the Saturday after the Epiphany the readings are eschatological texts from Isaiah 60-66 and Baruch. Readings remaining unused are omitted for that year.

150. During Lent the readings for the first year are passages from Deuteronomy and the Letter to the Hebrews. Those for the second year review the history of salvation from Exodus, Leviticus, and Numbers. The Letter to the Hebrews interprets the Old Covenant in the light of the paschal mystery of Christ. A passage from the same letter, on Christ's sacrifice (Heb 9:11-28), is read on Good Friday; another, on the Lord's rest (Heb 4:1-16), is read on Holy Saturday. On the other days of Holy Week the readings in Year I are the third and fourth Songs of the Servant of the Lord and extracts from Lamentations; in Year II the prophet Jeremiah is read, as a type of Christ in his passion.

151. During the Easter season, apart from the First and Second Sundays of Easter and the solemnities of the Ascension and Pentecost, there are the traditional readings from the First Letter of Peter, the Book of Revelation, and the Letters of John (for Year I), and from the Acts of the Apostles (for Year II).

---

7   Gregory the Great, *Homilia* 34 in *Evangelia*: PL 76: 1282.

152. From the Monday after the feast of the Baptism of the Lord until Lent and from the Monday after Pentecost until Advent there is a continuous series of thirty-four weeks in Ordinary Time.

This series is interrupted from Ash Wednesday until Pentecost. On the Monday after Pentecost Sunday the cycle of readings in Ordinary Time is resumed, beginning with the week after the one interrupted because of Lent; the reading assigned to the Sunday is omitted.

In years with only thirty-three weeks in Ordinary Time, the week immediately following Pentecost is dropped, in order to retain the readings of the last weeks, which are eschatological readings.

The books of the Old Testament are arranged so as to follow the history of salvation: God reveals himself in the history of his people as he leads and enlightens them in progressive stages. This is why prophetic books are read along with the historical books, but with due consideration of the period in which the prophets lived and taught. Hence, the cycle of readings from the Old Testament contains, in Year I, the historical books and prophetic utterances from the Book of Joshua as far as, and including, the time of the exile. In Year II, after the readings from Genesis (read before Lent), the history of salvation is resumed after the exile up to the time of the Maccabees. Year II includes the later prophets, the wisdom literature, and the narratives in Esther, Tobit, and Judith.

The letters of the apostles not read at special times are distributed through the year in a way that takes into account the readings at Mass and the chronological order in which these letters were written.

153. The one-year cycle is shortened in such a way that each year special passages from sacred Scripture are read, but in correlation with the two-year cycle of readings at Mass, to which it is intended to be complementary.

154. Proper readings are assigned for solemnities and feasts; otherwise the readings are taken from the respective Common of Saints.

155. As far as possible, each passage read keeps to a certain unity. In order therefore to strike a balance in length (otherwise difficult to achieve in view of the different literary genres of the books), some verses are occasionally omitted, though omissions are always noted. But it is permissible and commendable to read the complete passage from an approved text.

C. Short Readings

156. The short readings or "chapters" (*capitula*) are referred to in no. 45, which describes their importance in the liturgy of the hours. They have been chosen to give clear and concise expression to a theme or an exhortation. Care has also been taken to ensure variety.

157. Accordingly, four weekly series of short readings have been composed for Ordinary Time. They are incorporated into the psalter in such a way that the reading changes during the four weeks. There are also weekly series for the seasons of Advent, Christmas, Lent, and Easter. In addition there are proper short readings for solemnities, feasts, and some memorials, as well as a one-week series for night prayer.

158. The following determined the choice of short readings:

a. in accordance with tradition, exclusion of the Gospels;
b. respect for the special character of Sunday, or even of Friday, and of the individual hours;
c. use only of the New Testament for the readings at evening prayer, following as they do a New Testament canticle.

VII. READINGS FROM THE FATHERS AND CHURCH WRITERS

159. In keeping with the tradition of the Roman Church the office of readings has, after the biblical reading, a reading from the Fathers or

church writers, with a responsory, unless there is to be a reading relating to a saint (see nos. 228-239).

160. Texts for this reading are given from the writings of the Fathers and doctors of the Church and from other ecclesiastical writers of the Eastern and Western Church. Pride of place is given to the Fathers because of their distinctive authority in the Church.

161. In addition to the readings that *The Liturgy of the Hours* assigns to each day, the optional lectionary supplies a larger collection, in order that the treasures of the Church's tradition may be more widely available to those who pray the liturgy of the hours. Everyone is free to take the second reading either from *The Liturgy of the Hours* or from the optional lectionary.

162. Further, the conferences of bishops may prepare additional texts, adapted to the traditions and culture of their own region,[8] for inclusion in the optional lectionary as a supplement. These texts are to be taken from the works of Catholic writers, outstanding for their teaching and holiness of life.

163. The purpose of the second reading is principally to provide for meditation on the word of God as received by the Church in its tradition. The Church has always been convinced of the need to teach the word of God authentically to believers, so that "the line of interpretation regarding the prophets and apostles may be guided by an ecclesial and catholic understanding."[9]

164. By constant use of the writings handed down by the universal tradition of the Church, those who read them are led to a deeper reflection on sacred Scripture and to a relish and love for it. The writings of

---

8   See SC, art. 38.
9   Vincent of Lerins, *Commonitorium* 2: PL 50, 640.

the Fathers are an outstanding witness to the contemplation of the word of God over the centuries by the Bride of the incarnate Word: the Church, "possessing the counsel and spirit of its Bridegroom and God,"[10] is always seeking to attain a more profound understanding of the sacred Scriptures.

165. The reading of the Fathers leads Christians to an understanding also of the liturgical seasons and feasts. In addition, it gives them access to the priceless spiritual treasures that form the unique patrimony of the Church and provide a firm foundation for the spiritual life and a rich source for increasing devotion. Preachers of God's word also have at hand each day superb examples of sacred preaching.

VIII. READINGS IN HONOR OF SAINTS

166. The "hagiographical" readings or readings in honor of saints are either texts from a Father of the Church or another ecclesiastical writer, referring specifically or rightly applicable to the saint being commemorated, or the readings are texts from the saint's own writings, or are biographical.

167. Those who compose particular propers for saints must ensure historical accuracy[11] as well as genuine spiritual benefit for those who will read or hear the readings about the saints. Anything that merely excites amazement should be carefully avoided. Emphasis should be given to the individual spiritual characteristics of the saints, in a way suited to modern conditions; stress should also be laid on their contribution to the life and spirituality of the Church.

168. A short biographical note, simply giving historical facts and a brief sketch of the saint's life, is provided at the head of the reading. This is for information only and is not for reading aloud.

---

10   Bernard of Clairvaux, *Sermo 3 in vigilia Nativitatis* 1: PL 183 (ed. 1879) 94.

11   See SC, art. 92c.

IX. RESPONSORIES

169. Its responsory follows the biblical reading in the office of readings. The text of this responsory has been drawn from traditional sources or freshly composed, in order to throw new light on the passage just read, put it in the context of the history of salvation, lead from the Old Testament to the New, turn what has been read into prayer and contemplation, or provide pleasant variety by its poetic beauty.

170. A pertinent responsory also follows the second reading. It is less closely linked with the text of the reading, however, and thus makes for a greater freedom in meditation.

171. The responsories and the portions to be repeated even in private recitation therefore retain their value. The customary reprise of the whole responsory may be omitted when the office is not being sung, unless the sense requires this repetition.

172. In a similar but simpler way, the responsory at morning prayer, evening prayer, and night prayer (see nos. 49 and 89), and the verse at daytime prayer, are linked to the short reading as a kind of acclamation, enabling God's word to enter more deeply into the mind and heart of the one listening or reading.

X. HYMNS AND OTHER NONBIBLICAL SONGS

173. A very ancient tradition gives hymns the place in the office that they still retain.[12] By their mystical and poetic character they are specifically designed for God's praise. But they also are an element for the people; in fact more often than the other parts of the office the hymns bring out the proper theme of individual hours or feasts and incline and draw the spirit to a devout celebration. The beauty of their language often adds to this power. Furthermore, in the office hymns are the main poetic element created by the Church.

---

12   See SC, art. 93.

174. A hymn follows the traditional rule of ending with a doxology, usually addressed to the same divine person as the hymn itself.

175. In the office for Ordinary Time, to ensure variety, a twofold cycle of hymns is given for each hour, for use in alternate weeks.

176. In addition, a twofold cycle of hymns has been introduced into the office of readings for Ordinary Time, one for use at night and the other for use during the day.

177. New hymns can be set to traditional melodies of the same rhythm and meter.

178. For vernacular celebration, the conferences of bishops may adapt the Latin hymns to suit the character of their own language and introduce fresh compositions,[13] provided these are in complete harmony with the spirit of the hour, season, or feast. Great care must be taken not to allow popular songs that have no artistic merit and are not in keeping with the dignity of the liturgy.

XI. INTERCESSIONS, LORD'S PRAYER, AND CONCLUDING PRAYER

A. The Prayers or Intercessions at Morning Prayer and Evening Prayer

179. The liturgy of the hours is a celebration in praise of God. Yet Jewish and Christian tradition does not separate prayer of petition from praise of God; often enough, praise turns somehow to petition. The Apostle Paul exhorts us to offer "prayers, petitions, intercessions, and thanksgiving for all: for kings and all in authority, so that we may be able to live quiet and peaceful lives in all reverence and decency, for this is good and acceptable before God our Savior, who wishes all to be saved and to come to the knowledge of the truth" (1 Tm 2:1-4). The

---

13   See SC, art. 38.

Fathers of the Church frequently explained this as an exhortation to offer prayer in the morning and in the evening.[14]

180. The general intercessions, restored in the Mass of the Roman Rite, have their place also at evening prayer, though in a different fashion, as will be explained later.

181. Since traditionally morning prayer puts the whole day in God's hands, there are invocations at morning prayer for the purpose of commending or consecrating the day to God.

182. The word *preces* covers both the intercessions at evening prayer and the invocations for dedicating the day to God at morning prayer.

183. In the interest of variety and especially of giving fuller expression to the many needs of the Church and of all people in relation to different states of life, groups, persons, circumstances, and seasons, different intercessory formularies are given for each day of the four-week psalter in Ordinary Time and for the special seasons of the liturgical year, as well as for certain feasts.

184. In addition, the conferences of bishops have the right to adapt the formularies given in the book of the liturgy of the hours and also to approve new ones,[15] in accordance with the norms that follow.

185. As in the Lord's Prayer, petitions should be linked with praise of God and acknowledgment of his glory or with a reference to the history of salvation.

186. In the intercessions at evening prayer the last intention is always for the dead.

---

14   Thus, for example, John Chrysostom, *In Epist. ad Tim 1*, Homilia 6: PG 62, 530.
15   See SC, art. 38.

187. Since the liturgy of the hours is above all the prayer of the whole Church for the whole Church, indeed for the salvation of the whole world,[16] universal intentions should take precedence over all others, namely, for: the Church and its ministers; secular authorities; the poor, the sick, and the sorrowful; the needs of the whole world, that is, peace and other intentions of this kind.

188. It is permissible, however, to include particular intentions at both morning prayer and evening prayer.

189. The intercessions in the office are so arranged that they can be adapted for celebration with a congregation or in a small community or for private recitation.

190. The intercessions in a celebration with a congregation or in common are thus introduced by a brief invitation, given by the priest or minister and designating the single response that the congregation is to repeat after each petition.

191. Further, the intentions are phrased as direct addresses to God and thus are suitable for both common celebration and private recitation.

192. Each intention consists of two parts; the second may be used as an alternative response.

193. Different methods can therefore be used for the intercessions. The priest or minister may say both parts of the intention and the congregation respond with a uniform response or a silent pause, or the priest or minister may say only the first part of the intention and the congregation respond with the second part.

---

16   See SC, art. 83 and 89.

B. Lord's Prayer

194. In accord with ancient tradition, the Lord's Prayer has a place suited to its dignity, namely, after the intercessions at morning prayer and evening prayer, the hours most often celebrated with the people.

195. Henceforth, therefore, the Lord's Prayer will be said with solemnity on three occasions during the day: at Mass, at morning prayer, and at evening prayer.

196. The Lord's Prayer is said by all after a brief introduction, if this seems opportune.

C. Concluding Prayer

197. The concluding prayer at the end marks the completion of an entire hour. In a celebration in public and with a congregation, it belongs by tradition to a priest or deacon to say this prayer.[17]

198. In the office of readings, this prayer is as a rule the prayer proper to the day. At night prayer, the prayer is always the prayer given in the psalter for that hour.

199. The concluding prayer at morning prayer and evening prayer is taken from the proper on Sundays, on the weekdays of the seasons of Advent, Christmas, Lent, and Easter, and on solemnities, feasts, and memorials. On weekdays in Ordinary Time the prayer is the one given in the four-week psalter to express the character of these two hours.

200. The concluding prayer at daytime prayer is taken from the proper on Sundays, on the weekdays of the seasons of Advent, Christmas, Lent, and Easter, and on solemnities and feasts. On other days the prayers are those that express the character of the particular hour. These are given in the four-week psalter.

---

17   See no. 256 of this Instruction.

XII. SACRED SILENCE

201. It is a general principle that care should be taken in liturgical services to see that "at the proper times all observe a reverent silence."[18] An opportunity for silence should therefore be provided in the celebration of the liturgy of the hours.

202. In order to receive in our hearts the full sound of the voice of the Holy Spirit and to unite our personal prayer more closely with the word of God and the public voice of the Church, it is permissible, as occasion offers and prudence suggests, to have an interval of silence. It may come either after the repetition of the antiphon at the end of the psalm, in the traditional way, especially if the psalm-prayer is to be said after the pause (see no. 112), or after the short or longer readings, either before or after the responsory.

Care must be taken to avoid the kind of silence that would disturb the structure of the office or annoy and weary those taking part.

203. In individual recitation there is even greater freedom to pause in meditation on some text that moves the spirit; the office does not on this account lose its public character.

---

18   SC, art. 30.

CHAPTER IV
Various Celebrations Throughout the Year

I. MYSTERIES OF THE LORD

A. Sunday

204. The office of Sunday begins with evening prayer I, which is taken entirely from the four-week psalter, except those parts that are marked as proper.

205. When a feast of the Lord is celebrated on Sunday, it has a proper evening prayer I.

206. The way to celebrate Sunday vigils, as circumstances suggest, has been discussed in no. 73.

207. It is of great advantage to celebrate, when possible, at least evening prayer with the people, in keeping with a very ancient tradition.[1]

B. Easter Triduum

208. For the Easter triduum the office is celebrated in the way set forth in the Proper of Seasons.

209. Those who take part in the evening Mass of the Lord's Supper or the celebration of the Lord's passion on Good Friday do not say evening prayer on either day.

---

1   See SC, art. 100.

210. On Good Friday and Holy Saturday the office of readings should be celebrated publicly with the people before morning prayer, as far as this is possible.

211. Night prayer for Holy Saturday is said only by those who are not present at the Easter Vigil.

212. The Easter Vigil takes the place of the office of readings. Those not present at the solemn celebration of the Vigil should therefore read at least four of its readings with the chants and prayers. It is desirable that these be the readings from Exodus, Ezekiel, St. Paul, and from the Gospel. The *Te Deum* follows, then the prayer of the day.

213. Morning prayer for Easter Sunday is said by all. It is fitting that evening prayer be celebrated in a more solemn way to mark the ending of so holy a day and to commemorate the occasions when the Lord showed himself to his disciples. Great care should be taken to maintain, where it exists, the particular tradition of celebrating evening prayer on Easter Sunday in honor of baptism. During this there is a procession to the font as the psalms are being sung.

C. Easter Season
214. The liturgy of the hours takes on a paschal character from the acclamation, *Alleluia* that concludes most antiphons (see no. 120), from the hymns, antiphons, and special intercessions, and from the proper readings assigned to each hour.

D. Christmas Season
215. On Christmas eve it is fitting that by means of the office of readings, a solemn vigil be celebrated before Mass. Night prayer is not said by those present at this vigil.

216. Morning prayer on Christmas Day is said as a rule before the Mass at Dawn.

E. Other Solemnities and Feasts of the Lord

217. In arranging the office for solemnities and feasts of the Lord, what is said in nos. 225-233 should be observed, with any necessary changes.

II. THE SAINTS

218. The celebrations of the saints are arranged so that they do not take precedence over those feast days and special seasons that commemorate the mysteries of salvation.[2] Nor are they allowed to break up the sequence of psalms and biblical readings or to give rise to undue repetitions. At the same time, the plan makes proper provision for the rightful honoring of the individual saints. These principles form the basis for the reform of the calendar, carried out by order of Vatican Council II, and for the plan for celebrating the saints in the liturgy of the hours that is described in the following paragraphs.

219. Celebrations in honor of the saints are either solemnities, feasts, or memorials.

220. Memorials are either obligatory memorials or, when not so classified, optional memorials. In deciding on the merits of celebrating an optional memorial in an office to be celebrated with the people or in common, account should be taken of the general good or of the genuine devotion of the congregation, not simply that of the person presiding.

221. When more than one optional memorial falls on the same day, only one may be celebrated; the rest are omitted.

222. Only solemnities are transferred, in accordance with the rubrics.

223. The norms that follow apply to the saints entered in the General Roman Calendar and to those with a place in particular calendars.

---

2   See SC, art. 111.

224. Where proper parts are not given, they are supplied from the respective Common of Saints.

1. Arrangement of the Office for Solemnities

225. Solemnities have an evening prayer I on the preceding day.

226. At evening prayer I and II, the hymn, the antiphons, the short reading with its responsory, and the concluding prayer are proper. Where anything proper is missing, it is supplied from the common.

In keeping with an ancient tradition, at evening prayer I both psalms are as a rule taken from the *Laudate* Psalms (Ps 113, 117, 135, 146, 147 A, 147 B). The New Testament canticle is noted in its appropriate place. At evening prayer II the psalms and canticles are proper; the intercessions are either proper or from the common.

227. At morning prayer, the hymn, the antiphons, the short reading with its responsory, and the concluding prayer are proper. Where anything proper is missing, it is supplied from the common. The psalms are to be taken from the Sunday of Week I of the four-week psalter; the intercessions are either proper or from the common.

228. In the office of readings, everything is proper: the hymn, the antiphons and psalms, the readings and the responsories. The first reading is from Scripture; the second is about the saint. In the case of a saint with a purely local cult and without special texts even in the local proper, everything is taken from the common.

At the end of the office of readings the *Te Deum* and the proper prayer are said.

229. At daytime prayer, the hymn of the weekday is used, unless other directions are given. The psalms are from the Gradual Psalms with a proper antiphon. On Sundays the psalms are taken from the Sunday of

Week I of the four-week psalter and the short reading and concluding prayer are proper. But on certain solemnities of the Lord there are special psalms.

230. At night prayer, everything is said as on Sundays, after evening prayer I and II respectively.

2. Arrangement of the Office for Feasts

231. Feasts have no evening prayer I, except those feasts of the Lord that fall on a Sunday. At the office of readings, at morning prayer, and at evening prayer, all is done as on solemnities.

232. At daytime prayer, the hymn of the weekday is used. The weekday psalms with their antiphons are said, unless a special reason or tradition requires a proper antiphon; this will be indicated as the case occurs. The reading and concluding prayer are proper.

233. Night prayer is said as on ordinary days.

3. Arrangement of the Office for Memorials

234. In the arrangement of the office there is no difference between obligatory and optional memorials, except in the case of optional memorials falling during privileged seasons.

A. Memorials During Ordinary Time

235. In the office of readings, at morning prayer, and at evening prayer:

    a. the psalms and their antiphons are taken from the current week and day, unless there are proper antiphons or proper psalms, which is indicated as the case occurs;

    b. the antiphon at the invitatory, the hymn, the short reading, the antiphons at the Canticles of Zechariah and of Mary, and the intercessions must be those of the saint if these are given in the proper; otherwise, they are taken either from the common or from the current week and day;

c. the concluding prayer from the office of the saint is to be said;

d. in the office of readings, the Scripture reading with its responsory is from the current cycle. The second reading is about the
saint, with a proper responsory or one taken from the common; if there is no proper reading, the patristic reading for the
day is used. The *Te Deum* is not said.

236. At daytime prayer and night prayer, all is from the weekday and
nothing is from the office of the saint.

B. Memorials During Privileged Seasons

237. On Sundays, solemnities, and feasts, on Ash Wednesday, during
Holy Week, and during the octave of Easter, memorials that happen to
fall on these days are disregarded.

238. On the weekdays from 17 to 24 December, during the octave of
Christmas, and on the weekdays of Lent, no obligatory memorials are
celebrated, even in particular calendars. When any happen to fall during Lent in a given year, they are treated as optional memorials.

239. During privileged seasons, if it is desired to celebrate the office of
a saint on a day assigned to his or her memorial:

a. in the office of readings, after the patristic reading (with its
responsory) from the Proper of Seasons, a proper reading
about the saint (with its responsory) may follow, with the concluding prayer of the saint;

b. at morning prayer and evening prayer, the ending of the concluding prayer may be omitted and the saint's antiphon (from
the proper or common) and prayer may be added.

C. Memorial of the Blessed Virgin Mary on Saturday

240. On Saturdays in Ordinary Time, when optional memorials are permitted, an optional memorial of the Blessed Virgin Mary may be celebrated in the same way as other memorials, with its own proper reading.

III. CALENDAR AND OPTION TO CHOOSE AN
OFFICE OR PART OF AN OFFICE

A. Calendar to be Followed

241. The office in choir and in common is to be celebrated according to the proper calendar of the diocese, of the religious family, or of the individual churches.[3] Members of religious institutes join with the community of the local Church in celebrating the dedication of the cathedral and the feasts of the principal patrons of the place and of the wider geographical region in which they live.[4]

242. When clerics or religious who are obliged under any title to pray the divine office join in an office celebrated in common according to a calendar or rite different from their own, they fulfill their obligation in respect to the part of the office at which they are present.

243. In private celebration, the calendar of the place or the person's own calendar may be followed, except on proper solemnities and on proper feasts.[5]

B. Option to Choose an Office

244. On weekdays when an optional memorial is permitted, for a good reason the office of a saint listed on that day in the Roman Martyrology, or in an approved appendix to it, may be celebrated in the same way as other memorials (see nos. 234-239).

245. For a public cause or out of devotion, except on solemnities, the Sundays of the seasons of Advent, Lent, and Easter, Ash Wednesday, Holy Week, the octave of Easter, and 2 November, a votive office may be celebrated, in whole or in part: for example, on the occasion of a pilgrimage, a local feast, or the external solemnity of a saint.

---

3   See General Norms for the Liturgical Year and the Calendar, no. 52.

4   See ibid., no. 52c.

5   See ibid., Table of Liturgical Days, nos. 4 and 8.

C. Option to Choose Texts

246. In certain particular cases there is an option to choose texts different from those given for the day, provided there is no distortion of the general arrangement of each hour and the rules that follow are respected.

247. In the office for Sundays, solemnities, feasts of the Lord listed in the General Calendar, the weekdays of Lent and Holy Week, the days within the octaves of Easter and Christmas, and the weekdays from 17 to 24 December inclusive, it is never permissible to change the formularies that are proper or adapted to the celebration, such as antiphons, hymns, readings, responsories, prayers, and very often also the psalms.

In place of the Sunday psalms of the current week, there is an option to substitute the Sunday psalms of a different week, and, in the case of an office celebrated with a congregation, even other psalms especially chosen to lead the people step by step to an understanding of the psalms.

248. In the office of readings, the current cycle of sacred Scripture must always be respected. The Church's intent that "a more representative portion of the holy Scriptures will be read to the people in the course of a prescribed number of years"[6] applies also to the divine office.

Therefore the cycle of readings from Scripture that is provided in the office of readings must not be set aside during the seasons of Advent, Christmas, Lent, and Easter. During Ordinary Time, however, on a particular day or for a few days in succession, it is permissible, for a good reason, to choose readings from those provided on other days or even other biblical readings: for example, on the occasion of retreats, pastoral gatherings, prayers for Christian unity, or other such events.

249. When the continuous reading is interrupted because of a solemnity or feast or special celebration, it is allowed during the same week, taking

---

6   SC, art. 51.

into account the readings for the whole week, either to combine the parts omitted with others or to decide which of the texts are to be preferred.

250. The office of readings also offers the option to choose, with a good reason, another reading from the same season, taken from *The Liturgy of the Hours* or the optional lectionary (no. 161), in preference to the second reading appointed for the day. On weekdays in Ordinary Time and, if it seems opportune, even in the seasons of Advent, Christmas, Lent, and Easter, the choice is open for a semicontinuous reading of the work of a Father of the Church, in harmony with the biblical and liturgical context.

251. The readings, prayers, songs, and intercessions appointed for the weekdays of a particular season may be used on other weekdays of the same season.

252. Everyone should be concerned to respect the complete cycle of the four-week psalter.[7] Still, for spiritual or pastoral advantage, the psalms appointed for a particular day may be replaced with others from the same hour of a different day. There are also circumstances occasionally arising when it is permissible to choose suitable psalms and other texts in the way done for a votive office.

---

7   See nos. 100-109 of this Instruction.

CHAPTER V
Rites for Celebration
in Common

I. OFFICES TO BE CARRIED OUT

253. In the celebration of the liturgy of the hours, as in all other liturgical services, "each one, minister or layperson, who has an office to perform, should do all of, but only, those parts which pertain to that office by the nature of the rite and the principles of liturgy."[1]

254. When a bishop presides, especially in the cathedral, he should be attended by his college of priests and by ministers, and the people should take a full and active part. A priest or deacon should normally preside at every celebration with a congregation, and ministers should also be present.

255. The priest or deacon who presides at a celebration may wear a stole over the alb or surplice; a priest may also wear a cope. On greater solemnities the wearing of the cope by many priests or of the dalmatic by many deacons is permitted.

256. It belongs to the presiding priest or deacon, at the chair, to open the celebration with the introductory verse, begin the Lord's Prayer, say the concluding prayer, greet the people, bless them, and dismiss them.

257. Either the priest or a minister may lead the intercessions.

---

1   SC, art. 28.

258. In the absence of a priest or deacon, the one who presides at the office is only one among equals and does not enter the sanctuary or greet and bless the people.

259. Those who act as readers, standing in a convenient place, read either the long readings or the short readings.

260. A cantor or cantors should intone the antiphons, psalms, and other chants. With regard to the psalmody, the directions of nos. 121-125 should be followed.

261. During the gospel canticle at morning prayer and evening prayer there may be an incensation of the altar, then of the priest and congregation.

262. The choral obligation applies to the community, not to the place of celebration, which need not be a church, especially in the case of those hours that are celebrated without solemnity.

263. All taking part stand during:

    a.   the introduction to the office and the introductory verses of each hour;
    b.   the hymn;
    c.   the gospel canticle;
    d.   the intercessions, the Lord's Prayer, and the concluding prayer.

264. All sit to listen to the readings, except the gospel.

265. The assembly either sits or stands, depending on custom, while the psalms and other canticles (with their antiphons) are being said.

266. All make the sign of the cross, from forehead to breast and from left shoulder to right, at:

a. the beginning of the hours, when *God, come to my assistance* is being said;

b. the beginning of the gospel, the Canticles of Zechariah, of Mary, and of Simeon.

The sign of the cross is made on the mouth at the beginning of the invitatory, at *Lord, open my lips.*

II. SINGING IN THE OFFICE

267. In the rubrics and norms of this instruction, the words "say," "recite," etc., are to be understood to refer to either singing or recitation, in the light of the principles that follow.

268. "The sung celebration of the divine office is more in keeping with the nature of this prayer and a mark of both higher solemnity and closer union of hearts in offering praise to God. . . . Therefore the singing of the office is earnestly recommended to those who carry out the office in choir or in common."[2]

269. The declarations of Vatican Council II on liturgical singing apply to all liturgical services but in a special way to the liturgy of the hours.[3] Though every part of it has been revised in such a way that all may be fruitfully recited even by individuals, many of these parts are lyrical in form and do not yield their fuller meaning unless they are sung, especially the psalms, canticles, hymns, and responsories.

270. Hence, in celebrating the liturgy singing is not to be regarded as an embellishment superimposed on prayer; rather, it wells up from the depths of a soul intent on prayer and the praise of God and reveals in a full and complete way the community nature of Christian worship.

---

2   SCR, Instr. MusSacr, 5 March 1967, no. 37. See also SC, art. 99.

3   See SC, art. 113.

Christian communities of all kinds seeking to use this form of prayer as frequently as possible are to be commended. Clerics and religious, as well as all the people of God, must be trained by suitable catechesis and practice to join together in singing the hours in a spirit of joy, especially on Sundays and holydays. But it is no easy task to sing the entire office; nor is the Church's praise to be considered either by origin or by nature the exclusive possession of clerics and monks but the property of the whole Christian community. Therefore several principles must be kept simultaneously in mind if the sung celebration of the liturgy of the hours is to be performed correctly and to stand out in its true nature and splendor.

271. It is particularly appropriate that there be singing at least on Sundays and holydays, so that the different degrees of solemnity will thus come to be recognized.

272. It is the same with the hours: all are not of equal importance; thus it is desirable that those that are the true hinges of the office, that is, morning prayer and evening prayer, should receive greater prominence through the use of singing.

273. A celebration with singing throughout is commendable, provided it has artistic and spiritual excellence; but it may be useful on occasion to apply the principle of "progressive solemnity." There are practical reasons for this, as well as the fact that in this way the various elements of liturgical celebration are not treated indiscriminately, but each can again be given its connatural meaning and genuine function. The liturgy of the hours is then not seen as a beautiful memorial of the past demanding intact preservation as an object of admiration; rather it is seen as open to constantly new forms of life and growth and to being the unmistakable sign of a community's vibrant vitality.

The principle of "progressive solemnity" therefore is one that recognizes several intermediate stages between singing the office in full and just reciting all the parts. Its application offers the possibility of a rich and pleasing variety. The criteria are the particular day or hour being celebrated, the character of the individual elements comprising the office, the size and composition of the community, as well as the number of singers available in the circumstances.

With this increased range of variation, it is possible for the public praise of the Church to be sung more frequently than formerly and to be adapted in a variety of ways to different circumstances. There is also great hope that new ways and expressions of public worship may be found for our own age, as has clearly always happened in the life of the Church.

274. For liturgical celebrations sung in Latin, Gregorian chant, as the music proper to the Roman liturgy, should have pride of place, all other things being equal.[4] Nevertheless, "the Church does not exclude any type of sacred music from liturgical services as long as the music matches the spirit of the service itself and the character of the individual parts and is not a hindrance to the required active participation of the people."[5] At a sung office, if a melody is not available for the given antiphon, another antiphon should be taken from those in the repertoire, provided it is suitable in terms of nos. 113 and 121-125.

275. Since the liturgy of the hours may be celebrated in the vernacular, "appropriate measures are to be taken to prepare melodies for use in the vernacular singing of the divine office."[6]

276. But it is permissible to sing the various parts in different languages at one and the same celebration.[7]

---

4   See SC, art. 116.
5   SCR, Instr. MusSacr, no. 9. See also SC, art. 116.
6   SCR, Instr. MusSacr, no. 41; see also nos. 54-61.
7   See ibid., no. 51.

277. The decision on which parts to choose for singing follows from the authentic structure of a liturgical celebration. This demands that the significance and function of each part and of singing should be fully respected. Some parts by their nature call for singing:[8] in particular, acclamations, responses to the greetings of priest and ministers, responses in litanies, also antiphons and psalms, the verses and reprises in responsories, hymns, and canticles.[9]

278. Clearly the psalms are closely bound up with music (see nos. 103-120), as both Jewish and Christian tradition confirm. In fact a complete understanding of many of the psalms is greatly assisted by singing them or at least not losing sight of their poetic and musical character. Accordingly, whenever possible singing the psalms should have preference, at least for the major days and hours and in view of the character of the psalms themselves.

279. The different ways of reciting the psalms have been described in nos. 121-123. Varying these ways should depend not so much on external circumstances as on the different genres of the psalms to be recited in the same celebration. Thus the wisdom psalms and the narrative psalms are perhaps better listened to, whereas psalms of praise and thanksgiving are of their nature designed for singing in common. The main consideration is to ensure that the celebration is not too inflexible or elaborate nor concerned merely with formal observance of rules, but that it matches the reality of what is being celebrated. The primary aim must be to inspire hearts with a desire for genuine prayer and to show that the celebration of God's praise is a thing of joy (see Ps 147).

280. Even when the hours are recited, hymns can nourish prayer, provided they have doctrinal and literary excellence; but of their nature

---

8   See ibid., no. 6.
9   See ibid., nos. 16a and 38.

they are designed for singing and so, as far as possible, at a celebration in common they should be sung.

281. The short responsory after the reading at morning prayer and evening prayer (see no. 49) is of its nature designed for singing and indeed for congregational singing.

282. The responsories following the readings in the office of readings by their very nature and function also call for their being sung. In the plan of the office, however, they are composed in such a way that they retain their power even in individual and private recitation. Responsories set to simpler melodies can be sung more frequently than those responsories drawn from the traditional liturgical books.

283. The longer readings and the short readings are not of themselves designed for singing. When they are proclaimed, great care should be taken that the reading is dignified, clear, and distinct and that it is really audible and fully intelligible for all. The only acceptable melody for a reading is therefore one that best ensures the hearing of the words and the understanding of the text.

284. Texts that are said only by the person presiding, such as the concluding prayer, can be sung gracefully and appropriately, especially in Latin. This, however, will be more difficult in some languages, unless singing makes the texts more clearly audible for all.